THE ANGELUS TRANSCRIPTS

2013–2014

Emrayel A'a Ra iry a'a

Copyright © 2019 Emrayel A'a Ra iry a'a.

All rights reserved. No part of this book may be used or reproduced by any means, graphic, electronic, or mechanical, including photocopying, recording, taping or by any information storage retrieval system without the written permission of the author except in the case of brief quotations embodied in critical articles and reviews.

Because of the dynamic nature of the Internet, any web addresses or links contained in this book may have changed since publication and may no longer be valid. The views expressed in this work are solely those of the author and do not necessarily reflect the views of the publisher, and the publisher hereby disclaims any responsibility for them.

The author of this book does not dispense medical advice or prescribe the use of any technique as a form of treatment for physical, emotional, or medical problems without the advice of a physician, either directly or indirectly. The intent of the author is only to offer information of a general nature to help you in your quest for emotional and spiritual well-being. In the event you use any of the information in this book for yourself, which is your constitutional right, the author and the publisher assume no responsibility for your actions.

Any people depicted in stock imagery provided by Getty Images are models, and such images are being used for illustrative purposes only. Certain stock imagery © Getty Images.

Contents

Preface xv
Introduction xvii

The Journal: Year 2013

May 20, 2013 1
June 12, 2013 2
July 10, 2013 4
July 22, 2013 6
August 3, 2013 7
August 10, 2013 9
September 15, 2013 11
September 25, 2013 13
October 1, 2013 15
October 1, 2013 17
October 11, 2013 18
October 13, 2013 19
October 17, 2013 21
October 23, 2013 22
October 26, 2013 24
October 29, 2013 25
November 17, 2013 27
November 23, 2013 29
November 29, 2013 30
December 5, 2013 32
December 7, 2013 34
December 9, 2013 36
December 10, 2013 39

December 12, 2013 42
December 13, 2013 44
December 14, 2013 46
December 15, 2013 48
December 16, 2013 50
December 21, 2013 53
December 22, 2013 55
December 25, 2013 57
December 26, 2013 59
December 27, 2013 61
December 28, 2013 64
December 31, 2013 67

The Journal: Year 2014

January 3, 2014 73
January 5, 2014 76
January 8, 2014 80
January 9, 2014 81
January 25, 2014 83
January 26, 2014 86
January 27, 2014 87
January 31, 2014 90
February 3, 2014 92
February 5, 2014 94
February 9, 2014 96
February 16, 2014 98
February 16, 2014 100
February 18, 2014 101
March 6, 2014 104
March 11, 2014 106
March 12, 2014 107
March 12, 2014 110
March 19, 2014 111
March 21, 2014 112
March 22, 2014 114

March 27, 2014	117
April 2, 2014	118
April 2, 2014	119
April 11, 2014	122
April 16, 2014	125
April 22, 2014	129
April 24, 2014	132
April 25, 2014	135
April 27, 2014	137
April 28, 2014	138
May 2, 2014	140
May 3, 2014	142
May 4, 2014	145
May 8, 2014	148
May 10, 2014	151
May 13, 2014	154
May 14, 2014	158
May 15, 2014	159
May 18, 2014	161
May 19, 2014	163
May 20, 2014	164
May 23, 2014	167
May 25, 2014	170
May 27, 2014	173
May 28, 2014	175
May 29, 2014	176
June 1, 2014	178
June 2, 2014	181
June 6, 2014	183
June 9, 2014	186
June 12, 2014	188
June 15, 2014	191
June 17, 2014	194
June 19, 2014	196
June 20, 2014	198

June 23, 2014	201
June 26, 2014	202
June 27, 2014	203
June 30, 2014	206
June 30, 2014	207
July 1, 2014	210
July 2, 2014	212
July 3, 2014	214
July 4, 2014	215
July 6, 2014	217
July 6, 2014	220
July 6, 2014	221
July 7, 2014	222
July 8, 2014	223
July 8, 2014	224
July 9, 2014	225
July 9, 2014	227
July 10, 2014	229
July 11, 2014	230
July 12, 2014	231
July 13, 2014	232
July 13, 2014	234
July 14, 2014	237
July 15, 2014	238
July 16, 2014	239
July 16, 2014	240
July 18, 2014	241
July 18, 2014	242
July 19, 2014	245
July 19, 2014	246
July 20, 2014	247
July 21, 2014	248
July 21, 2014	249
July 22, 2014	250
July 23, 2014	251

July 24, 2014 253
July 25, 2014 254
July 25, 2014 257
July 26, 2014 259
July 27, 2014 260
July 28, 2014 262
July 28, 2014 263
July 29, 2014 264
July 30, 2014 265
July 30, 2014 267
July 31, 2014 272
August 1, 2014 273
August 2, 2014 274
August 2, 2014 275
August 3, 2014 277
August 4, 2014 278
August 5, 2014 279
August 6, 2014 280
August 6, 2014 281
August 7, 2014 282
August 7, 2014 283
August 8, 2014 284
August 9, 2014 285
August 10, 2014 286
August 10, 2014 287
August 11, 2014 289
August 11, 2014 290
August 12, 2014 291
August 12, 2014 293
August 13, 2014 294
August 13, 2014 295
August 14, 2014 296
August 14, 2014 297
August 14, 2014 298
August 15, 2014 299

August 15, 2014 300
August 15, 2014 303
August 16, 2014 304
August 17, 2014 305
August 17, 2014 307
August 18, 2014 308
August 19, 2014 309
August 20, 2014 310
August 21, 2014 311
August 21, 2014 312
August 21, 2014 313
August 22, 2014 314
August 23, 2014 315
August 24, 2014 316
August 25, 2014 317
August 26, 2014 318
August 26, 2014 319
August 27, 2014 320
August 28, 2014 322
August 29, 2014 323
August 30, 2014 324
August 30, 2014 325
August 30, 2014 327
August 31, 2014 328
August 31, 2014 329
August 31, 2014 330
August 31, 2014 334
September 1, 2014 336
September 2, 2014 337
September 3, 2014 338
September 4, 2014 339
September 5, 2014 340
September 6, 2014 341
September 7, 2014 342
September 7, 2014 343

September 8, 2014 345
September 9, 2014 346
September 10, 2014 347
September 11, 2014 348
September 12, 2014 349
September 13, 2014 350
September 14, 2014 351
September 15, 2014 352
September 16, 2014 353
September 17, 2014 354
September 18, 2014 355
September 19, 2014 357
September 20, 2014 359
September 20, 2014 360
September 21, 2014 364
September 22, 2014 365
September 22, 2014 367
September 23, 2014 370
September 24, 2014 371
September 25, 2014 372
September 26, 2014 373
September 27, 2014 374
September 28, 2014 375
September 29, 2014 376
September 30, 2014 377
October 1, 2014 378
October 2, 2014 379
October 3, 2014 380
October 4, 2014 381
October 5, 2014 382
October 6, 2014 383
October 7, 2014 385
October 8, 2014 386
October 8, 2014 387
October 9, 2014 391

October 10, 2014 392
October 11, 2014 393
October 12, 2014 394
October 13, 2014 395
October 14, 2014 396
October 15, 2014 397
October 16, 2014 398
October 17, 2014 399
October 18, 2014 400
October 19, 2014 401
October 20, 2014 403
October 21, 2014 404
October 22, 2014 405
October 23, 2014 407
October 24, 2014 409
October 25, 2014 411
October 26, 2014 412
October 27, 2014 414
October 28, 2014 415
October 29, 2014 416
October 30, 2014 417
October 31, 2014 418
November 1, 2014 419
November 2, 2014 420
November 3, 2014 422
November 4, 2014 424
November 5, 2014 425
November 6, 2014 426
November 7, 2014 427
November 8, 2014 428
November 9, 2014 429
November 10, 2014 430
November 11, 2014 432
November 12, 2014 433
November 13, 2014 434

November 14, 2014 435
November 15, 2014 436
November 16, 2014 437
November 17, 2014 438
November 18, 2014 439
November 19, 2014 440
November 20, 2014 441
November 21, 2014 443
November 22, 2014 445
November 23, 2014 446
November 24, 2014 447
November 25, 2014 448
November 26, 2014 450
November 27, 2014 451
November 28, 2014 453
November 29, 2014 454
November 30, 2014 456
December 1, 2014 457
December 2, 2014 459
December 3, 2014 460
December 4, 2014 461
December 5, 2014 464
December 6, 2014 465
December 7, 2014 467
December 8, 2014 469
December 9, 2014 470
December 10, 2014 471
December 11, 2014 473
December 12, 2014 474
December 13, 2014 475
December 14, 2014 476
December 15, 2014 477
December 16, 2014 479
December 18, 2014 482
December 19, 2014 484

December 20, 2014 486
December 21, 2014 487
December 22, 2014 489
December 23, 2014 491
December 24, 2014 493
December 25, 2014 495
December 26, 2014 496
December 27, 2014 498
December 28, 2014 499
December 29, 2014 501
December 30, 2014 503
December 31, 2014 504

Preface

This book is about the messages I have received from 2013 to 2014. Also included are the visions, art, and experiences I have had during those few years. These messages and experiences are a mixture of humour, wisdom, lessons, and growth. Some parts can be enlightening, and others are downright confusing. There you have my experiences in a nutshell. Many a time I have come away more confused than enlightened, only to find out a few days later what was meant.

The angels and I are like close friends. I trust them more than anyone can realise, and I love them without boundaries. They are my spiritual family. Through this friendship, they told me to write a journal. Well, this is part of that journal, and the angels wanted me to publish it.

A wee bit of info: the angels have a rather twisted sense of humour. So when you finally get to meet one, be prepared to be teased and made fun of, and to generally have the piss taken out of you. The best way to deal with this is to do the same back at them. They love it! Share your jokes and poke fun at each other. As I said, they love it. They fling it at me, and I fling back because my sense of humour is equally twisted.

The angels' humour may be warped, but there is nothing malicious about it. It's more mischief than anything. When you return that humour, it is best to keep the humour in the same vein.

They love it!

Enjoy it, and you will find that they're very funny and will have you laughing often. Your vibrations will rise higher with the fun.

Let it be known that I do not control what they say or edit it. What they tell me is what they want me to write down. Spelling mistakes are totally my own. If what they say is disturbing at times, it is meant to make you think on your path. In other words, a warning of possible events that may occur if you take the wrong path. They do this because they don't want you to lose your path into the light.

Does this blurb help to clarify some matters? I hope so.

Introduction

Let's talk a bit about what I do.

I channel the angels. I either do it directly from the source, or I use the angel tarot cards if I'm a bit tired. Now, I'm not dependent on the tarot cards because I can do these readings without them if I feel inclined.

The channelling happens when the angel merges with my body and takes over my voice. The message is either spoken out loud or related to me via telepathy. Either way, I always have my hands free during the channelling so as to type down what message I am reading.

With spirit guides, mine do the same thing. They merge with my body and speak through me. With other people's spirit guides, I hear them and sometimes see them, but they don't merge with me.

Quite often this is the time I do my artwork.

My relationship with the angels is that I treat them like they are part of my family.

Michael is very much the big brother to me and is just as protective. Haniel mothers me a bit, but I don't mind. Uriel acts as a father with me.

I get on with them all, but the ones I get on best with are Gabriel (my teacher), Emmanuel (friend and guide), and Azrael. Lately, Cassiel has been coming through to me, and I now know that he likes to hug.

Mainly I consider them my other family, and they know it. We all have our moments when we banter with each other, but there's no malice there, just fun and love.

How did it all begin with me?

I was born with my psychic abilities, and I was lucky to have a mother who was open to the spirit world. She encouraged me throughout my life to use my abilities and wouldn't let anyone try to shut me down. Some child psychologists who didn't understand were quickly pushed out by my mother.

I grew up in Gateshead, which is on the banks of the River Tyne, opposite Newcastle-upon-Tyne. Yes, in good ol' north-east England, where the Geordie accent was thicker than a political candidate and the streets were dirtier than a coal mine.

Life was rough, and in the sixties if you were the slightest bit different from the others, you got hassled unmercifully. Yes, I was different from the other kids and got bullied quite a lot. The teachers at various schools I went to couldn't figure me out and so called in the child psychologists. That was when it was found out I had a very high IQ of 145 and was ahead of the other children.

I kept hidden my other differences.

As I grew older, these hidden differences of mine began to show: I became a member of Mensa because of my IQ level. Also, my abilities began to grow. I began to show signs of Telekinesis. A speaker that was firmly hooked on a wall one evening was found the next day across the room. For it to move, it had to move upwards from the hook and be carried to its landing spot. Personal items began to vanish and then reappear a few hours later in the same spot where several people had searched before.

My abilities it grew from there.

If my description of my childhood appears vague, it is because I can barely remember my childhood. That part of my life appears to mostly missing, so I can assume it wasn't a very happy one and that my mind has decided it wasn't worth remembering.

A few years back, I was alone in the house and began to see a shadow person wandering about the place. The house was new, and I was the first person to live in it. This shadow person began to hassle me every night and through the night. I did the usual cleansings and banishings, but they lasted only a few days. The shadow person soon came back, and the feelings of fear from it became stronger.

Even in broad daylight, I would stare down the hallway and see this black mass floating a few yards away from me. Then it would slowly fade away. Can't get more obvious than that!

It turned out that the portal that this spirit was coming through was in one of the bedrooms. In the end, it was getting too much, and I called a medium who was experienced in these matters. She told me how to open a portal, banish the spirit, and close the portal. She also gave me details on another type of cleansing.

I soon felt the spirit coming back to hassle me again that night. I decided to talk to the spirit on the spiritual plane, and soon it was apologising for frightening me. We agreed that it needed to curb down on the fear factor, and I'd see what I could do to help.

Soon it came to me, fear levels low. I spoke of what it was like beyond the white light and how beautiful it was there. Soon the shadow person backed off, and I sensed thought coming from it.

Two days later it was back, and there was no fear at all. That was the clue that it wanted to go to the light. I opened the portal for the spirit and called a beloved family member of his to come through. I sensed happiness, and the spirit passed through.

As soon as I did this, I felt a pair of arms wrap around me and hug me. Yes, my guides and guardian angels were very pleased with me. I then closed my own portal. That was when I also sealed the spirit portal in the other bedroom.

I have video footage of an orb coming out of this portal, circling it, and then shooting off at speed to the living room, where I was sitting at the time.

The spirit never came back.

The medium I had spoken to earlier on I got in contact again and explained what had happened. That was when I was invited to a development circle, and it became apparent I had strong abilities but needed training.

One thing leads to another.

I was at the local spiritualist church at the time as a psychic artist, and it was part of my training to do podium work. This can be rather boring if the spirits decide they don't want to talk with me. I tuned into spirit to see who my first spirit visitor was for me to sketch. Tuning into spirit was difficult for me because they seem to be on a different level as to what I can access. I can access the higher levels because my vibrational energy is of the higher levels. I must smother my energy a bit to reach the lower levels. This can be awkward because it feels like I'm crippling myself.

I couldn't feel any spirit yet but could sense energy. I then felt the urge to draw a picture. I whisked out my pad and a pencil and started drawing. The only emotion I felt from the energy was anticipation.

As I sketched the facial outlines, the energy began to show a face in my third eye, and so I had to draw the face on the pad. It was a beautiful face. There was also a message, which I wrote down, but I have not related here because it is a private message for someone else.

At the end of the message, it signed off as Raphael.

That is how my first contact with the angels went.

Raphael visited me for a few more times to prepare me, and then Gabriel took over and began to train me for angel channelling. As time went on, I got stronger. I'm still growing here. He told me that this had been my destiny since the beginning and that they had been waiting for the right time.

I was also told that Raphael came to me to see if I could receive him yet because he considered me ready. He did this a few more times, and I received him. This was the trigger that started the training.

How do I see angels?

I rarely see sparks or flickering lights. I don't see angels as shadows, but I do see them as moving, nearly transparent, glowing forms through my third eye.

Archangel Michael is peering over my shoulder as I type this.

I feel intense emotions from them, which are mainly love or laughter. What I sense from Michael right now is curiosity, amusement, and love.

As for hearing them, it's like a whisper that gets louder as I go deeper into a trance state. If I'm wide awake, then I can still hear them as a whisper. But mainly it's through telepathy that they speak to me. That is the easiest and best because it is so clear.

I was like most mediums and would channel passed ones, but Raphael chose me to pass a message through—twice. That this sequence of events triggered in me an urge to say out loud, "I dedicate myself to the angels, for whatever purpose the angels wish for me to be." This was the start, and the angels took me up on that willingly.

Since then, they have used me as their messenger.

The catalyst is to offer yourself to the angels unconditionally. They will take you up on that offer, but don't be surprised if they use you in a capacity other than what you expected. They know what you are best at and will use that ability. They will even enhance it if it is your destiny. If you want to be a healer but have a strong ability for clairvoyance that you didn't know of, they will make sure you know of it quick. They did with me. The angels will enhance that ability and help it grow, and you can't ignore it. It becomes the main part of your abilities.

I wanted to be a healer because I was strong in that area. I didn't know I was also a very strong clairvoyant and clairaudient until the angels got their hands on me. Now those abilities are the mainstay of my life.

They opened me to the world of the angels and have shown me their world.

Beautiful!

Anyway, enough of my ramblings. Let's get this show on the road.

The Journal: Year 2013

May 20, 2013

Last night, I went to bed and tried to sleep. Note the word *tried*. Instead, I found myself sinking into a deep, meditative trance.

I had a vision that I was in this open space with plants and trees surrounding a glade. Standing around me were archangels. I couldn't see their features. They appeared as tall beings made of pure light and had humanlike forms, but I saw no details.

One behind me seemed to be explaining me to the others. Now, I don't know what was said because it appeared to be a silent conversation among them. They then all turned towards me, and I got the impression that they "looked" at me. The one behind me finished the explanation, turned, and said something to me that I can't remember. Then it took me to a place that had lots of plants.

The angel showed me what they saw through their eyes. I sensed a feeling of amusement and mischief from the angel. The angel told me his name: Gabriel. Soon after that, I was taken back to my body and bed.

I roused out of this trance and wondered, *For what reason did the archangels want me there?* I suspected that in time, I would find out.

***

June 12, 2013

Oh, my! I've been told I must pass on a message. I have no choice but to do so, and you will soon see why.

A Message from Archangel Raphael

The time has come for you all to look at yourselves and see what you have done that was worthwhile.

Did you help someone in trouble?
Did you lend a helping hand to someone who needed it?
Did you give your love to someone who wanted it?

Take a good look and consider this: we are all equal in the eyes of God—all of us! God is not Jewish, God is not Muslim, and God is not Christian. God is all! God is love! So consider this and judge yourself instead of judging others by your own petty, materialistic standards.

It saddens me when bigotry, hate, and ignorance ruin innocent lives. What have these innocents done to deserve this? They didn't do anything. So please look to yourselves and remove this negativity. It serves no purpose but to lower your levels to the point of self-destruction. Instead of using a fist, caress a cheek with an open hand. Stroke a loved pet.

Please take note of my words, for you will have to judge yourselves when your time has come.

Archangel Raphael

***

July 10, 2013

A Message

Let it be that the light of the Divine comes to you.
Let it be that the light enters you from above and pours into your soul.
Let it be that you become one with the light.
Let it be that you become the light and part of the Divine.
Let it be that you ascend into the realm of the beloved.

The beloved ones are the people who have risen above all worldly ways and have become perfect. This is a wondrous thing to aspire to.
Please heed the wisdom of these ascended ones. They have lived the same lives as you have and risen above them. They have become one with the light. They are blessed indeed. They too wish to help humanity and work with us. So please do not fear to speak to us, as fear serves no purpose. Instead, use love with your words. We hear and see your words and feelings. We will heed your request. Though you may think we aren't doing anything, we are. But you just haven't noticed the subtle way we work. Never ask us to hate, for it is not a part of us, and we will not give what is of the darkness.

You are safe with us, and we will help you, but you just must ask with love in your hearts. And all we ask in return is your love. Please heed my words, which I say with love for you all. We are here to help. We are only a thought away.

I will now thank my messenger for passing my words to you all.

Archangel Michael

***

July 22, 2013

Message to All

It saddens me to see what people do to each other. They seek to destroy each other for nothing. This should not be! You were all made for a higher purpose, and nothing negative should get in the way of that. Instead, I see the negative being embraced by some people. Do you realise this is painful to your spirit? Stop and look within you, feel your inner self, and you will find your soul crying. This is a fault of weakness within yourself, so don't blame others for your failings. You have free will and have chosen your path. But you can also choose to step off that path and move onto a new path.

If you want to travel onto your new path to the light, please call upon us angels because we will help you—but only with your permission. Each can help in many subtle and infinite ways. The power bestowed on these angels is immense yet gentle. We only want to serve and help.

Call us, ask us, and love us. In turn, we hear, we answer, and we love back.

I thank my messenger.

Gabriel

***

August 3, 2013

Message Time from a Certain Archangel

The time has come for you to make up your minds as to what you need in your lives. Do you want to walk with us in the light? Or do you want to sit and wait for the light to notice you finally?

If you chose to sit and wait, you would find that the time spent waiting is wasted. The light will not seek you out if you sit and expect everyone and everything to come to you. It's all a matter of life on the physical plane. If you want to go forward, you must take the first steps. Sitting and waiting means you will be left behind. Simple as that. If you chose to walk with us, then the light would see you the quickest, for if we are to gain knowledge and wisdom, we must seek it. That too is a matter of life here.

And when the light sees you, you will feel the blessings of the Divine, and you will feel the Divine's love like we do.

Walk with us in the full glow of the Divine light. And let us all embrace the Divine's love for us all. It nurtures, it pleases, and it is wonderful. Will you unite and walk towards the Divine light? If you do, we will make the path easy for your steps and we will help you on the way. All you need to do is ask us. That is all. Nothing is too big or too small. Just ask us with love in your hearts, and we will reply in our subtle ways—also with love.

I know for a fact that if we embrace you with our love, you can feel it. We also know that once you have felt this love, you want it more. We have love to give. Come walk the path to enlightenment, and join us in our walk in the light.

Love and light.

I thank my messenger.

Gabriel

***

August 10, 2013

A New Message from an Archangel I Spoke with Once Before

I hear all, and I see all. I hear your calls for help, but unless you give me permission, I cannot help. If you want my help, ask me and give me permission to help you. Then nothing in your world can stop me from helping you. The only time I will not help is if you want to harm another person. That is not my function and is abhorrent to me.

If you want my love, I give it freely; just ask.
If you want me to help you to help another, just ask.
If you want me to give you confidence during uncertainty, just ask.
If you want me to save you when you are surrounded by darkness, just ask.

Just have a higher purpose in your heart and ask me. I will help. Do not demand, for that is negative. One gets more results with honey than vinegar. Honey is the love; vinegar is the hate.
Fill your soul with the honey of love, and I will help you.

If you want me to send your love to others, gladly I will help; your love is perfect to the Divine and me. I feel that love you gave, and I will add my love to it. That is what the Divine considers as part of the light. Love is eternal, and my payment for helping you is just your gratitude and love.

I am of the light and of love. Blessed be!

Michael

***

September 15, 2013

A Message from Archangel Gabriel

As you sail on the waves of the universe, feel the ripples that rock the boat. Feel the storm that brews from afar. You have the oars, you have the tiller, and you can steer away from it. This is what your fate and destiny are in life. This is how you can move through the seas of your life.

Steer the boat of your life towards the harbour of sanctuary. The light that glows at the harbour is for you. It is your lighthouse of safety. Steer that boat towards the lighthouse and take shelter under this light. The light will protect you, nurture you, and love you, for it is the Divine light. The Divine light will guide you safely through storms and tempests that will try to distract you from your path.

That is what the sea of your life is like. The Divine is your goal towards perfection; the storms are what others put in your path to stop you. Avoid the storms and head towards the Divine. Let the Divine's light show you the way and let us help in protecting you. That is our task: to watch, to wait, and to help you when you call upon us. We are your friends, we are your spirit brothers, and we are your beloved. You are our friends, you are our physical brothers, and you are our beloved too.

My beloved ones heed my words and let us help you in finding the Light among your stormy world. Call us if you need us. Call us with love and gratitude. We will answer.

All this for the simple reason: love, love, and most important Divine love.

Thank you for hearing me.

Gabriel

***

September 25, 2013

A Rare Message from My Guardian Angel

The little things in life are to be treasured. They are many and yet they are few—those little things such as flowers, fish, the animals and the birds. They are many, but they are becoming few. Please don't harm their lives and their homes, but in turn nurture these creatures. They too are part of the grand design that is called life in this world. Believe me, so are you.

Every form of life is related to you if you go back far enough. For in the beginning, you were all one. In harming these creatures, you are harming yourselves. Don't do that, please. You are too precious to be lost this way. The Divine has plans for you and what a plan it is. It is magnificent and humbling, yet so simple. Love the creatures and plants in this world as you would love yourself. You all started off as one creature, and you will all eventually end in the form of another—a form that is so beautiful and magical. You will have a form that is perfection.

Think about this and respect the world you are living on, Gaia is worthy of such. Love her in all her forms, and she in turn will love you without restraint. The creatures and plants are her children. You too are her children, so don't run from her.

Gaia gives herself unstintingly to you, but you turn from her often. This saddens her, and often you don't listen. By all your mining and destroying her forests, you are creating more harm than good. She is starting to feel the first signs of pain. Be aware if you don't stop, she will take steps to remove the cause. You may be her children, but she will sacrifice the few to save the many. Remember, flora and fauna are her children too, and they outnumber you. Please be gentle, love her, cherish her, talk to her, laugh with her, and share these gifts with her other children. She will respond back lovingly with many rewards.

I thank you for listening to me, my loves. And I hope you have learnt something. I shall leave you now.

Fleur

***

October 1, 2013

Message

Let there be love in your light. Let there be joy in your love. Join us now with reverence, love, and laughter because this is what the Divine enjoys the most. Be one with us, and don't let anyone take away your joy. Don't let them take away your love and happiness. They are yours to enjoy and yours only. If anyone tries to get in the way of your happiness, then leave them behind. They have their path, so don't let them try to knock you off yours.

Be at peace within yourself, as that inner peace comes from forgiving all that have hurt you. As soon as you let go of these negative influences, they will open the way to lighter more pleasant feelings. The inner peace can help you reach the stars and beyond. The ecstasy that you feel will be the one provided to you by the Divine. Love the Divine. Love the love we give you.

If you feel as if no one wants you, lonely, or withdrawn, remember you are not alone and never will be alone. We will be around. We will watch over you. We will listen. We will love you. We will care for you. Just call out to us, and we will always hear you. Believe me when I say that. We will never turn you away but will welcome you.

I say this to my messenger also, who is feeling lost. You are never alone and will always be close to us. Don't forget you are one of many who has the same feelings. Be at peace because you have already seen my message to the others. This too is for you. Yes, you indeed heard my signal to you earlier on.

Be well, all of you. Be well. Be blessed, and we will watch over you. I leave you now.

Chamuel

****

(Note: Chamuel had such overpowering loving energy that it nearly sent my mind into a trance state. As soon as he left, I broke down into a crying mess.)

***

October 1, 2013

My own thoughts.

What is it like to be able to channel the archangels? At times it's fantastic, and sometimes it's scary because you just don't know whom or what you're going to get, or when it's going to happen. Their energy can be soothing, or it could just about blast you out of your seat.

They happen at random, and yes, they do nag you when they want to talk to you. They nag by signs or pictures bearing their name. You even hear their name in your head when you are relaxing. All you can do is wait until you find the right time and spot to relax in. The archangels are patient and are quite willing to wait for your right moment.

What all the books and messages from other mediums failed to prepare me for was their sense of humour. Their humour is good-natured, gentle, and mischievous. Yes, Gabriel caught me off guard with one of his jokes, but I can honestly say it was a very pleasant experience.

I rarely see them, but I feel their presence and hear their messages. The only time I see them is when I draw them. Have you ever been hugged by an archangel? Gabriel did that to me, and it's an experience that I will never forget. It was beautiful!

Interesting, unusual, engrossing.

***

October 11, 2013

Last night I was pondering on the reason why Chamuel was visiting me so often and wanting me to pass on his messages. I asked this question out loud to myself, and I heard a voice in my ear: "He loves you!"

I perked out of my ruminations and felt a presence near me. I got the image of Michael sitting not far from me and watching. Now, he's the only archangel that whispers in my ear. The others just say what they want in my head.

Intrigued, I started asking light questions, such as whether the other archangels that I haven't spoken with yet use me as their voice. The answer to that was that they would in time. Gradually we ended up having idle chit-chat. The impression was that he was giving me some time to get to know him better. He was friendly, humorous, and cracking the odd joke.

I enjoyed our moment of time.

***

October 13, 2013

Message

We who have waited for a long time are pleased to be introduced to you. We are Haniel and Raguel. We have come to you in love and in the Light to pass on this message. A message you will find of interest.

Be aware of the changes that are happening around the world, for they are small aspects of the big plan. What appears to be a war is nothing more than the manifestation of these changes affecting people's minds. Some can accept and work with these changes; others cannot, and chaos is the result. It is your job to focus on these events and remove the darkness that is the cause of this chaos. We will help you with guidance and energy, but the concentration and actions are all to be yours. This is your test and your trial. Pass this, and the next level will be introduced.

This next level is different; you will relish it for what it is. It is that of love, harmony, faith, and life. In this level, you will then take your love and give it to every living creature that grows, crawls, or even takes root on the earth. You will become the guardians of life that we all hope you will take on. This is the journey of light; take this journey and feel how right it is. This journey is of personal and public growth. As you develop and create harmony in your world, you are creating harmony within flora and fauna.

This is the next level of perfection, and many of you are becoming aware of it. This is because you have reached the doorway and are awaiting it to be opened. Bide a while outside this door as we are waiting for more to come to it. You will not go through this door alone because it is a job that takes many, not one. And you will delight in this new task and companionship. Bear this current world a bit longer, and all will become clear. The next steps in harmony are yours to take, and only you can take them. We cannot do this for you, but we can guide you to them. You only have to ask.

We await your next steps with interest and with joy.

Be at peace with yourself, for it is within yourself that the first step is taken.

I thank you and our messenger.

Haniel and Raguel

***

October 17, 2013

An interesting moment last night during a group session. The conversation steered towards what the others had experienced in the past during their pursuit of mediumship.

While I was sitting and listening to this conversation, I felt the energy to the right of me. I recognised it as Gabriel, but I said nothing to the others and waited to see if the others would notice. My right hand was on the armrest of the chair, and I felt Gabriel's hand gently hold mine. His words came into my head that he was simply observing the others. We had a quick chat, and then we both remained silent and listened.

***

October 23, 2013

I had an interesting experience last night. You know I'm a clairaudient and clairsentient. During meditation, I found myself in a glade at night, and it was surrounded by trees. But the ground where I was standing on was made of pure light. I sat on the ground and noticed I was wearing a robe that was lapis coloured.

I sat on this ground, and a spirit being approached from outside the glade, watching me. It had no features. I felt no danger, but it never came close. I welcomed it, and then it backed off. Soon after, another being approached the outside of the glade and watched me. This one had features, and it was of a very handsome man. He pointed to the ground in front of me. I welcomed him and looked at where he was pointing.

I saw the light make a space, and a small pedestal of rocks and stones appeared. The rocks moved and made shapes, and the light appeared in the cracks. The cracks made the light shift into geometric shapes and forms. This was when I knew who this man was. It was Archangel Metatron. Every time he appears to me, he gets closer and my abilities take a boost. Then he left.

Later that day, I was awake and receiving healing. During this session, I saw a lovely, elegant lady from the late 1930s, dressed in a rose-pink fishtail gown that had black sequins on it. Her hair was blonde and in a bun. As soon as she saw me looking at her, she smiled, and we started to communicate. I asked her to show off her dress to me, and she did. She danced all over the place, having the time of her life. I got the impression that she wanted me to pass on to my healer that she was young again, healthy, dancing her heart out, and having fun.

I told my healer, and the response was that the lady was a dear friend of her and her aunt, and she had died just four to five months ago.

Yes! I've now developed clairvoyancy, which I've always wanted. To Metatron, I thank you with all my love.

***

October 26, 2013

Oh, dear! My attempts to stay positive and happy has taken a beating lately. My job insecurities caught up with me when I was very tired. I was feeling down in the dumps this morning and a bit crabby. All were heading towards a bit of the blues and a tad of self-pity. Next thing I knew, there was an energy nudging in me, and so I opened my senses.

The result: I got well and truly told off by Archangel Haniel and got a lecture to boot. But all in all, I was told that my medium abilities are my full-time job and that I was to leave all my worries and problems to them because they had control of them. I should stop putting myself down and to take more rest.

I shall consider myself told off. Haniel wasn't angry with me, just stern and loving. Did you know that the angels consider us humans as naughty but lovable children? One of my guides is amused by this.

***

October 29, 2013

A message just came in from Archangel Jeremiel.

> Welcome, my friends. Welcome! You have come so far in your lives so to be with us. I assure you that things are moving ahead, and you never need to worry. We will take care of it.
>
> This is a time of personal growth and enlightenment, and it is your time. Learn about the world about you, and learn of its magic, its love, and its future carers: you! Learn to love, appreciate others, and let others love and appreciate you. It's all giving and taking out in your world. You give love, and you take it back threefold. All will be right in your world, and you will be right in yourself.
>
> Beloved, let those who come into your life bearing gifts of love and light become your life. Love and light are the most important and powerful things in the universe, and it is because it is directly from the Divine. This won't take long, and you can help love move along everyone else by simply giving it. You are made of love, and you are made with love. Don't worry about what others try to do to destroy that love within you; it cannot die. The Divine knows that and will do everything to protect that part of you. It is your spark, your light, your real self. It is you!

You belong with us in love, and the light belongs with you. Combined, you are powerful, you are wondrous, and you are the Divine's promise. Embrace your inner self with all the external quirks and faults; they are what help you towards pureness. As one experiences dark moments, they help you to appreciate the moments of light.

Go out there in your world, go in peace, and go with love. Be in the light and be part of the light. You have that gift; you are made with that gift inside you. Never let others try to take it away from you, because your part of the light is for you only. The others have theirs, but they are wanting more than their fair share and seek yours. They will soon learn their greed will hold them back in their incarnations.

Believe me when I wish the light and love to flow through you, for it is a magnificent sight and the purest feeling you will ever experience.

Be well, and never let your faith and belief to fail. Keep it strong, and you will leap over any obstacles placed in your path.

It is done, and so is my message. I love you all. I love my messenger for passing on my words.

I am Jeremiel.

Thank you!

***

November 17, 2013

Well, I've just come back from the spiritualist church. The angels have been preparing the way for my next steps without letting me know. A series of events did warn me, but I failed to realise their import.

Clue 1. As soon as I walked into the gate, I was informed that the guest medium hadn't turned up and that I was on the podium. I remarked that I had spoken to the guest medium, and he had confirmed he was coming.

Clue 2. The guest medium still hadn't turned up at the start of service. It was all run by ear, and routine went out the window. I rang the guest medium to find he had the times wrong and was going like the clappers to get where I am.

Clue 3. My stand for my easel to rest on had disappeared, so no colour spirit artwork could be done. Only pencil art could be done on my lap. That was quickly done.

Clue 4. A feeling that I needed to help came upon me, and so I tuned in, felt a presence join me. It kept me in a light trance state, even though I was aware and could move and stand up. This made me offer to do the inspirational message.

Yep! I ended up being up in front of everyone. I passed on the message, which I can barely remember. But I remember who the presence is that channelled through me: dear, sweet Gabriel.

After this, I was shaking with nerves, and the song that was played after that was very apt because it mentioned angel voices.

I've just recently been told by Gabriel that everything had been arranged that way, including the lateness of the guest medium, to get me up front. The angels decided that it was time that I move forward, and they gave me a spiritual kick in the pants.

***

November 23, 2013

An interesting moment today as I had a catnap. As I was dozing, I felt a presence near me, and I then heard a voice in my head say, "Now is the time for your ascendency."

I roused at that and felt puzzled by what those words meant.

Soon I went back into my doze, and Raphael came to visit. I can't remember as to what was said, but I do remember asking him for some healing for someone, and he agreed. I remember thanking him, and then I roused up again.

I'm still feeling a bit airy-fairy a few hours after I've woke up. Something must have happened because this only happens during a deep meditative state, and I normally can balance myself within a few seconds. Not this time.

***

November 29, 2013

A message just came in from Archangel Michael. While receiving this message, I had the urge to smile and laugh.

> Listen to me. Let the world know your strength and your light. Show the world that you are part of love and part of us. Bring your light forward and show the world who you are. This is what your next step is. The light is not only from the Divine but is also from you. Therefore, show the world your light, and in doing so, you are showing the world the glory of the Divine.
>
> Isn't it great that we all can do this? Wonderful, in fact! You are blessed in this as we are all for one aim in sight: the aim for unity and love. That is the most beautiful thing in the world. Don't worry about the wars and famine. They are already being taken care of by us. We have heard your pleas and requests to stop the suffering, and so we are working on that now.
>
> Let us sing not only for the pleasure of it but also for the joy it brings to yourself and others. Singing and dancing are all expressions of this. While you do this, your frequency rises, and this brings you nearer to us and easier for us to contact you. We like that a lot! This aids in communication with us and helps us in our mutual work of peace.

Belong in the light with our blessing. We will never forsake you all. You have our undying friendship and love. Be well and be free. And if you want something? Well, you know the routine. Just ask. We won't run away, I promise you. We have no fear of you, and you don't need to fear us. Believe me when I say you belong with us. For we are, in a way, one. No more, no less.

Now, remember. Have fun, laugh, sing, dance, joke. and even show love. It's all good and positive.

Be at peace and be with love.

I thank you all, and I thank my messenger.

Michael

***

December 5, 2013

A message just came in right now.

> Be the time that is in your life. Be the essence of the life of this world.
>
> Let it be that you are one of many, but you have many followers of the one that is you. Don't let others put you down, and don't let them lead you away from your own path. You have yours, and they have theirs. Part the ways and go ahead in your life.
>
> You wish to know of many things, but mainly you wish to know of your own future. Well, I can see that future, and you will be amazed at what I have seen. It is wonderful. It is grand. Your future has many promises and many opportunities. There will be a pitfall here and there, so don't worry about that. Learn from them. That's what they are there for. Your past is now nothing. You have acknowledged you have done wrong there; you have accepted the fact it is wrong. So you have forgiven yourself. Now go forward, my beloved. Go forward. You will learn and grow stronger with time, and we will help you. Go forward.
>
> We love you and always will, my beloved. Your path is long but has many adventures. But now it is time for you to grow. And grow you will.

Look forward to the days when you will talk with us more freely. You will hear us more clearly.

Be well, my friend, I am always with you in life and beyond. I love you with grace and with friendship. I am pleased with you, my voice. I am pleased.

Zadkiel

***

December 7, 2013

A message just came in right now when I asked if anyone had a message to pass. I felt the familiar surge of energy enveloping me inside and out.

>A message? Yes, I have a message.
>
>I call upon all of you lightworkers to unite and combine your strength in this time of flux. Be strong and be steadfast. Your strengths are needed to steady the energies. I ask of all of you to remain true to your selves and to each other. For in unity, you are the strongest of all. Your abilities are your strength. Raphael will come to those who call upon him for healing. Michael will come for those who ask for strength and steadfastness. Uriel will come to those who ask him for guidance, and Ariel for the wisdom of nature. They are your strengths; they are your friends in need. They are your friends indeed. We are your friends. I call upon you all to be our guiding lights for others to see you, to follow you, and to lead them to us. We will welcome all who turn to us in view of these guiding lights.
>
>Blessed are the lightworkers who aid us in the passing of our blessings and messages. We enjoy your company and your love. Your love is the most powerful thing in this world of yours. It is the harmony, it is strong, and it is your greatest asset. I

am thankful for your help and use of your abilities. I am pleased with how everyone has turned out.

My lightworkers, I love you all, and I give your task of bringing the light to others my blessing.

Be well, be blessed, and be my beloved friends.

I thank you, my friends. I thank you all.

Gabriel

***

December 9, 2013

A message to me that has come right now.

> There is a light at the end of the tunnel. And it's not a train coming in the opposite direction.
>
> Be patient; you will be rewarded soon Your problems will lessen. Time is for you to grow and learn. Both are the same in many ways, but you will learn. You have a lot more power than you realise, and I am going to teach you how to use it. Don't let the others stop you. They have less than you, and you need to learn this.
>
> Take heed of my words my friend. I will not lead you astray but will lead you further into the light. Your gift of speaking with us is one of many aspects. You can heal, you can see the future. You can even speak to those long passed into our realm. You can even move things with your mind. But you hide from some of these abilities. Well, hide no more. Time for you to learn and I'll make sure you will learn. This is the path that you need to take, and I rather have you come willingly than kicking and screaming.
>
> You have much to learn though, so be patient and be ready. Things are going to happen sooner than you think. I've always told you: Expect the unexpected. This still holds true. Your financial worries will be

taken care of, don't worry. All worry ever got you was a bad headache and a grumpiness.

Yes, Em, you feel my smile, and you know that I always love you. Give a little bit more time and when the time has arrived, look out world! Learn, and evolve. You are moving up and beyond. You weren't given the gift of hearing us for nothing; you were given this gift so that we may teach you with ease. Keep talking with us, and it will be easier, this I guarantee.

Now before I let you go, my sister. Hear this. There in the world are the crocodiles. Avoid the people who are these crocodiles, for they intend to prey on you, sapping your will and putting you down. Always keep in mind that I am always with you and will never let you down. I love you too much for that. The Divine loves you much also.

Now you know that soon you will begin your trip to ascendancy. You will learn much before you fully reach the first level. Learn well. I shall be watching and waiting. But I cannot help you with your path there, for it is your path and yours only. All I can do is advise and protect. Your decisions are yours alone. Either way, how it goes, I'll always be there for you.

Now enough is enough, and you're right, I am a bit of a chatterbox. Yes, you feel my laughter. I see your smile. I leave you now my sister.

Go forth and show your light. You have a great future ahead of you, and the world will know it. Zadkiel was right. Listen to his wise words.

Be love, be the light and be of the light. Love you.

Gabriel

***

December 10, 2013

My, another message come through, and through an archangel that I don't often get a chance to talk to, though I do love the energy of this angel.

Message from Azrael:

We all have life choices. And when we come to them, we must choose. That is what you all must do. No matter where you are from, that is your call. Crazy, isn't it? Sometimes when one needs a helping hand from beyond, we end up having to make a move on our own. So be it. That is how it is meant to be.

You have made your choices, and now you are walking the path of that choice. So far, you have shown promise, and I'm pleased for you and with you. You have shown willingness to learn. You picked up telekinesis very quickly. I am glad for that, though you consider it rather useless. It is not. It has taught you to focus your mind. Now, about the situation that you asked earlier in the day. Patience—always patience. Things will happen as they should. No faster or slower.

To the others who read my message, you too must be patient. All will come at the right time. No later, no earlier. Patience is a great virtue, and we set a lot by it. Wait with each other. You will be each other's strength. The more of you there are, the more that will unite together as one. You will part of that moment, the moment that all will be blessed with the Divine's love. That is the greatest gift of all.

Back to my voice now. Things happen for a reason, as you well know it. I agree with you when you say, "Why shouldn't it happen to me? There is no one more suitable to cope" during a crisis. You can cope, and you have done well in doing so. I had lent you my strength when times were rough, and you have held your head high. There are moments when you have faltered, but that happens to all. We all falter at moments. When this happens, learn from it so that you may know what to do when it happens again.

My friends, you too would be wise to heed my words there, for they are of relevance to you too. Accept the pratfalls and the face plants of life. They happen to teach you how to cope with them. When you have finally learnt the lesson, have a good laugh over the incident. This laughter will heal you quicker than sorrow.

Ah, I believe I have rambled on long enough, my friends. I am glad I can pass my message to you all to read. You know me as Azrael. In time you will get to know me better because I plan to talk more. I heard that, my voice. Your sense of humour is a joy to me, and I do not prattle on. I love you, my voice. I hope we have more conversations and perhaps some more laughter.

I will help you with your transition when the time comes.

With all my love,

Azrael

***

December 12, 2013

A few hours ago, this angel introduced itself to me. As I was busy doing other things, I asked it to have patience with me because I had things to do, and it agreed. Now I've sat down and said, "I'm ready for your message. You can take over."

And the angel did just that! A message just came in.

> I am Valeron. I wish you all well.
>
> You may not have heard of me, as I felt no need to introduce myself to most. I am going to pass my message on via the voice for the angels, my messenger here.
>
> I am the angel of goodwill and serenity. My message is that you have all come to my attention. Your goodwill, joy, and laughter have been sending signals up to the Divine that you are growing in number. That is wonderful. Now, please carry on the good work for the light. I love what you are doing, and I will follow you all. If you want peace and a clear head in a crisis, call upon me. If you wish to be forgiving and to embrace your enemy with love instead of malice, call upon me. I do forgiveness, as it is part of goodwill. I am more than willing to help you, but I need your permission to do this.
>
> I love the feeling of this Yuletide. The feeling of goodwill and joy is very pleasurable to us in our

realm. We look forward to this time also. We derive great pleasure watching you enjoy yourselves. Have fun, we all say, but do not hurt each other.

Remember there are those who are forgotten and have no one to share this celebration with. Why should they miss out on happiness and laughter? I see no reason at all, so I beg of you to think of these lonely ones and see fit within your heart to give a little something to them. A little gift will mean a lot to them in many, many ways.

Please think on this. I shall now take my leave of my messenger.

Thank you.

Valeron

During this entire message, I had felt a hand pressing on my head. Its energy was strong and pure. I got the impression of the colour of pale gold.

***

December 13, 2013

Another message from an archangel who has been quiet lately.

Hello, my friends. I am Chamuel, and I have a brief message that I wish to say.

I ask you to love yourselves as well as others. I ask that because the others are also part of yourselves. As you do to others, you do unto yourselves. That is the way it is supposed to be. It is the way of the light. It is the way of real love. It is also called karma by you.

Put down that gun and hold out an empty hand. Shake hands and embrace. Universal law demands that the fighting should stop; let the love begin. These are hard times, but only you can make it better. It will be an effort, but as I said, only you can change it.

Now, my beloved messenger, I will say this: Be well within yourself, and let love within your heart rule you for a while. Time for growth and time for contemplation is upon you. Learn, and you will learn at that. Change is starting to happen for you in a spiritual way, and it is showing. You are finding it easier to communicate with us, aren't you? That is the first sign. You now know when others are talking about you; you now hear them with your mind.

It is all part of your growth, and you are going to grow further. Beloved voice, we anticipate this growth within you. Expect the unexpected, as Gabriel tells you often. Gabriel loves you and will teach you.

Relax now and be with our love. I thank you for your time. Also, thank you for saying you love my energy. I've restrained it a bit because you said it was overpowering.

I love you all!

Right, let's go!

Bye-bye.

And just to stir the pot a bit, he gave me a surge of his energy, which nearly made me fall off my seat.

I must remember that the archangels have a sense of humour and will use every opportunity to use it!

***

December 14, 2013

Right now, I'm sitting at my desk and typing on my keyboard. I felt a gentle nudge, which meant someone wanted to pass a message. As I settled to do this, I felt a pair of arms wrap lovingly around me. It looks like this is going to be a good message.

Welcome, my dear friends.

I look at you all in this world, and I say to myself, "Joy is alive and well, and is in each of your hearts." That is wonderful. I like this. Well, it's time for you all to unite in mutual love and adoration of the Divine. The Divine is pleased by you all and wishes to bestow more love upon you all. Some may feel their spiritual gifts heightened at this time. Don't worry; it's all part of the big plan and should be welcomed.

Oh, my messenger has just reminded me that I have forgotten to introduce myself. I am Raphael, as if I needed reminding.

This surge of Divine love is the gift from all of us to you. Now is the time to move ahead in your development and learning. Take time to develop your new abilities and strengths. Make yourself familiar with them. If you have problems with them, just call for me, Michael, or Raziel. We will help you until you get on your feet again. Give thanks, love and gratitude to the Divine. The Divine will receive them with love.

And now a little something that has come to my attention. Believe in yourselves, all of you. You all have the promise to go to the limits and beyond. But the only thing that is stopping you is yourself. Shed old beliefs, worries, and preconceptions. Embrace our light with open arms, open minds, and open hearts. There is much to learn in your universe, so don't hold yourself back.

Thank you, beloved ones.

I wish you all well.

Raphael

During this message, Raphael placed his hand on my head. He's still here with me, hand still on my head, but just watching this time.

***

December 15, 2013

Well, I came back from the spiritualist church's Christmas party. No alcohol there—good! I occasionally join in this, though I normally don't have the time.

Anyway, they had some raffles going. I had supplied two of the prizes: a big plush bobcat and a reading. There was a prize I had an eye on, but someone took that.

Finally, it was reduced to the last prize left to win: the bobcat. They pulled out the winning ticket, and it had my name on it. Argh! Absolutely typical! The rest of the room thought my facial expression was hilarious because it was obvious that I didn't want the bobcat. Then their laughter turned hysterical when I told them I had donated the bobcat in the first place. Thankfully, another person and I did a swap.

While they all headed for the food, I started to suspect a trick had been played on me. I did a quick question about my guides, and they admitted they didn't do it, but they were amused at the situation. This quickly confirmed to me who had done it: dear, lovely Archangel Gabriel! I asked if he was the culprit, and he admitted to playing this joke on me. He was laughing.

I keep forgetting Gabriel loves playing harmless jokes on me. I'll get my own back.

I did a channelling of Gabriel at the party. The conversation had turned to the loss of loved ones and the different funeral arrangements in various countries. I felt Gabriel merge with me, and he appeared to be listening to the conversation and waiting. He left a message for everyone.

Pity I can't remember much about it because Gabriel takes over my voice completely, and I remain in a kind of light trance state. I must get a recorder!

***

December 16, 2013

Another message from an archangel I've never spoken to before. What calm and gentle energy I felt.

> I greet you all within the light of the Divine. I greet you all. I am Ariel. My message is to you all. Take care of the world you stand on, this world and all its inhabitants. This world is your only world in your current incarnation. Ruin that, and you ruin it for all future incarnations of yours and others. Protect the water, the land, the sea, the sky, the plants, the rocks, and the trees. The birds, fish, and all animals. This means you too. You are one of the many living creatures that walk in this world.
>
> There's a reason why this world is called Mother Earth.
>
> Yes, you are the children of this planet. So are all the other creatures that swim, crawl, fly, and walk upon the world. Plants are her children too. Love your world as much as you love yourself, and the rewards will be grand.
>
> It pains me when I see cruelty committed on others. It's not necessary, nor is it good. Such belongs to the darkness, not the light. We strive for perfection so that we grow into the light.

My beloved ones, please feel the forces of the world you are on. Feel the energies and the powers that flow through it. You are part of that energy and can tap into it. It's there, ready. This is the source of Mother Earth, and she nurtures you with that energy. Dearest ones, that energy is a form of love. Feel that love and give some of your own love back. Each will nurture the other. Many have done this, and many more will continue to do so. And as more and more of you lightworkers grow, the greater the world. This means the world will heal much faster.

My voice, you can relax now. Your time has come to look in other directions and grow. You are already feeling and sensing the changes happening in your own future. You will like what is going to happen. We will watch over you, protect you, and love you. You are beloved to us, as you are our voice. Yes, I know you can barely remember what we say. Don't worry; we will continue to use your voice to speak to others. Let others tell you what we said. You belong in the light, and you belong with the light. Look no further for inspiration or love. It is the ultimate in perfection. I will be here with my family, watching.

To all my readers, you too belong with the light. These words I say include you all. Let it be so and join each other under this light of love and divinity. The more that come to the light, the more your world will grow into the haven it is meant to be.

Be well, my readers, for I have passed on my message. You have all earned my love, and I must leave.

I give you my love and blessings.

Ariel

***

December 21, 2013

Chamuel wanted to pass this message.

> Well, it is that time of year again, when one's thoughts are turned to those who are no longer with you to celebrate this Yule. Let your thoughts dwell on these ones that are no moved on. Remember the happy times. Then celebrate their passing with joy, for they have reached another step towards perfection. Yule need not be a time of sadness or mourning; it is not supposed to be that way. It is a time of joy, celebration, and growth. Your loved ones are not far away, in fact. They are with you; your thoughts call them, and they listen. They came to you because they too wish to join in and celebrate.
>
> Remember this: your loved ones are only one step away from you. And they still love you. That can never change, and nor should it ever change.
>
> Be at peace with yourself and with others and celebrate this festivity. Let no one ever take away this time of love away from you. Be at peace indeed. That love is the most precious thing in this universe, and you have ready access to it. It is within you and around you. The Divine loves you, and so do we. We are never far away from you.
>
> Leave your cares and troubles behind and begin your celebration of growth and love this Yule. This is a

time that you will always treasure and remember, even those who think they have no one to celebrate it with have us.

We of the Divine realm treasure you all with love and hope. We will love you all unconditionally and with joy. We will give all the lightworkers our gift to you, our trust in you, and our love.

Be with this love and trust; it is within you all. This is what can bring love to you. And that love is widely spread across your world and to distant parts of the universe.

This is our Yule message for you. I wish you all the blessings of the Divine. And remember, you are never alone if you can feel our love.

Chamuel

***

December 22, 2013

Another message from an archangel with whom I really enjoy meeting.

> Well met, my friends.
>
> You are in a fine, joyful mood with the coming celebrations. That is good. Enjoy yourselves and do it on a grand scale. The more happiness you feel, the better it is for your health and your vibration. So go for it, but don't hurt anyone in doing so. As you say, karma will bite back thricefold.
>
> Let me introduce myself. I am Azrael. Yes, some of you heard my previous message, and I did say I'll be coming back to talk to you more often. Hmm? I sense your smile, my voice. I know you are happy to hear from me. That gladdens me.
>
> Anyway, we're drifting off the main point.
>
> My friends, don't forget those who have need of you. These are the people who have nothing. Though we are with them in celebration, it would help them if they had a little something from you all, be it a knitted hat that was made with love. That may be a small gift, but it's the thought and the love that counts. Even a gift as small as a packet of sweets is thought of love. Yes, as little as that. Love is more prized than money. Love is more precious than such

material things. Love is Chamuel's area of expertise and why am I rambling on about it? You all know what I mean.

The truth is, we archangels can feel love and give love. We can laugh with humour because laughter is part of the Light. We all can "meddle" with your lives, and we often do it in the name of love. We all want you to succeed and grow. And if we do a little tweak here and there, some call it synchronicity. My Voice calls it Serendipity.

Yes, my Voice, I'm quite aware I'm starting to wander off the path again. Why not! Now stop laughing at me as you are making me laugh. Ah my Voice, you give me joy. I, in turn, give you my love. For now, is the time for me to leave you. I shall remain watching and "meddling" as you call it.

My Light-Workers be blessed! The Divine has passed his love onto you and is proud of what you are trying to do. Be blessed and be rich in spirit, for you have deserved the greatest wealth of all, the enlightenment and spiritual growth of yourselves.

I love you all.

Azrael

***

December 25, 2013

Earlier, I was asking my guides about something, and I needed confirmation about a path change. My guides indicated yes. The angels told me to take this new path.

I told the angels that it would involve passing money for their words. Given that as their words were free of charge, I didn't want to charge others for the angel messages. Their reply was, "We shall see."

So, two confirmations. As I was asking for a third confirmation, I got this song rattling in my head. It's a country ballad, it has no name, and I suspect it hasn't been written yet. But the lyrics stuck in my mind.

> Don't let your dreams let you down.
> Don't stop them from chasing you around.
> Just stand still and believe
> For the gifts you're about to receive.
> Don't stop the world from turning by.
> Don't let your hopes fall and die.
> Just make your dreams become a fact,
> And the wonders you will attract.
>
> Chorus:
> How wonderful it is to be so beautiful.
> Your dreams are about to come true.
> Believe in yourself
> And get off that silly shelf.
> Follow your dreams, and they will follow you.

Just let the stars shine a light on you.
Show the world that the light is true.
Believe in us, and we will show
The direction you must go.
So take that step within your dreams.
Nothing is as bad as you believe it seems.
Open your heart and let us in.
Let the angels love you from within.

Chorus

Let the angels give you all their love.
Let in the light from far up above.
Believe in the light that's so true,
And take that path that you pursue.
It is the only true path you need to take,
From the heavens high to the deepest lake.
Believe in us and yourself, that is true,
For the Divine is within me and you.

Chorus

Copyright Heather Lennox, 2013

Interesting. I had wanted my third confirmation to be a white feather, but instead I got this song. It's now an earworm.

***

December 26, 2013

A little message from two angelic friends ...

Well, here I am. My greetings to everyone. This is my message at this interesting time of the year.

I greet you all with love and with my hand of friendship outstretched. I am Ariel. I've decided that you all need to have a quick think back on what I said in my previous message. Did anyone heed it? A lot of you did, and I was pleased. But there was the odd one or two who ignored it. That saddened me a bit. Then I thought, *They are still young. They will learn in time. Patience!*

I am pleased to say that you are all welcome in the eyes of the Divine. You are all welcome into the arms of the Divine. The Divine has nothing but love for those who are the followers of the light.

Now bear with me as I bring in another to pass a message.

I am Michael. Blessed are you all and my voice here. We have all followed your progress across the globe, and we are very pleased with you all.

To the caregivers and those who work selflessly for others so that you are all safe: I give my love and blessing.

To the lightworkers who shine their light of love nonstop on our behalf: I too bless you.

To those who have had a wonderful time these past few days: I bless you.

To those that have had no one to care for them and are forgotten: you have us beside you. We all bless you.

Yes, I bless each living creature in this world. Whether it walked, crawled, swam, flew, or flowered, I bless every living creature. Be blessed, my beloved friends. You are loved.

Voice, you do have a destiny to follow. You have asked us what you thought on a certain subject. All I will need to say is don't worry about it. Let us deal with our side of the bargain. You just go ahead and go for it.

Be well, my beloved friend. Time for change is now upon you. You are growing.

I thank you all.

Michael and Ariel

***

December 27, 2013

A loving message from Gabriel, my teacher.

Welcome, my dear friends. How are all of you coping with your celebrations? Some sore heads and some sore egos, I bet.

I am Gabriel, and I'm using my voice even further. This time I'm having a very active two-way conversation. She has grown since I have last spoken to her; this is expected.

Now, everyone, listen to me and I'll not mince words. Did you all do a good deed for someone who was lonely? I have read in my voice's mind that quite a few of you did, and I am very pleased. This is the moment to treasure what family you have left in this world and the friends and family who have gone on to the next. One touch, one word—that's how far these long gone are. Works in both living and long gone. Both can hear you quite well. I have a few surprises up my sleeve for you all, and my voice knows I like surprises. Even she doesn't know what they are. So be patient, and things will happen in their own time. And such good things that they are.

My lightworkers, now is the time for you to grow and expand your abilities, just like my voice has grown into a new ability. Our conversation can be heard by all who listen. She has a new path to follow, and

I am going to get her on it as it is meant to be. She'd better not drag her heels, or I'll drag her on it.

My voice, I would dare. Don't challenge me by saying I wouldn't dare, because I will! Give up and accept your new destiny. You will love it. And I dare because I love you. Anyway, I'm slipping off my path of thought worse than Azrael. I'm having a bit of fun there with him.

My lightworkers, be aware of these changes within you. Some of you are already feeling the effects of your new abilities and strengths. Some have yet to get there. To those I say, Be patient. Rome wasn't built in a day. You will get these new abilities, but only at the right time. You need to learn more before you get them. But of all these happenings that are all around you, just remember this: Take time for yourself. Rest is important and helps with your growth too. This means you as well my voice. Rest is important.

Everyone, as your abilities strengthen and develop, practice fine-tuning them. This means you will again strengthen them further. Don't overdo it, or I'll be very put out and must drag Raphael around to fix things. (Raphael's dry comment in the background: 'You would!')

So whether your celebration is for the birth of Christ or just for your own celebration of your own individual belief, either way you should rest often, learn often, and be yourself all the time.

Be at peace with yourself and with others. This is your time and your moment within that time. I bless you and leave you with my final message for the day.

May your God be with you always.

Gabriel

***

December 28, 2013

Here's a message from an archangel I've never spoken with before.

> Well, you have all done well.
>
> All of you, take time to relax. You've worked hard for this moment, so savour the rest from all the strife.
>
> Those with small very active children may find it easier to scream quietly.
>
> Relax now; time is slow at this moment.
>
> Throw away any useless and irritating thoughts and emotions.
>
> Take in a deep breath and let it out.
>
> Think of yourself surrounded by the Divine's white light of protection.
>
> Now breathe in and imagine yourself breathing in this white light.
>
> Hold your breath for a short while and then release it.
>
> Do this for approximately two minutes.
>
> Now, look within your own feelings. Do you feel different?

This is the feeling we want you to establish. It's called inner peace.

That is the feeling we all want you to have because it is such a wonderful, deep sensation. Enjoy it because it is pleasant.

There will be those out there that will not feel this or won't even try. That is because you cling to your negative feelings. You don't need to. Forgive those who have hurt you. That was in the past and is no longer valid. Forget those who prey on your mind. They are no longer part of your life, so let go.

Inner peace all starts when you start to forgive and forget. Think about my words.

Voice, stop worrying. You did the right thing. You will need your strength and your time now for your path. Don't let those others stop you. I am pleased to see you have taken this new path. We will help you with it now. As you are our voice, you are also our messenger. That is why Gabriel was chosen to talk to you. Ah, I see you are beginning to wonder who I am.

I am known by all as Uriel. I knew this was the time for me to talk to you. You have grown. You are part of the Divine's love, and you sit within his light. Beloved, you are more than what others think you are. You are more than what you think you are. In time you will be made aware of your gifts. Yes, gifts that you haven't touched yet because you haven't heard of them yet.

My lightworkers, the Divine is pleased with you and has asked me to say this to you: "Beloved ones, you are my pride and joy. You are the hope of humanity. Be strong, and my angels shall stand with you. I give you my love. Be well, and I love you all."

I too shall pass my love.

Be well within yourself.

Uriel

***

December 31, 2013

An end-of-year message from the loving Archangel Raphael.

Now is the time for you to let go of what negative things that have occurred in your year of 2013. This is the past we are talking about. Let go of any negative aspects, bad relationships, destroyed dreams, and heartbreak. Leave them behind because they will not serve you and never did. A new year is upon you, and so you must start afresh.

Think positively about not what has gone, but on what might happen. Think of these dreams of yours. Create new dreams and even think of new relationships if so desired. The more you think about what you really want, the bigger the chance of you receiving it. This has a simple name: manifestation. Manifest your dreams into reality. Plan on what you want and concentrate on it, step by step. We angels can read your minds, and things you think most of are our clues on what we need to do.

Do you want a parking space? Ask us, though we can do so much more. But then again, nothing is too little or too large for us. Just show us, tell us.

And when you feel the urge to go forward and make your dreams happen, you will find your path clear and without obstacles. We will even arrange for you to meet the people who can help you on that path.

Just be sure and confident in yourself and stride forward.

Did you know you have the capacity to make things happen just by will? You do, you know. The entire universe is within you because you are all part of that universe. The same energies that have created that universe are within you and at your beck and call. All you need to do is learn how to use them. Lightworkers know how to use a part of this energy. They use it to contact us, converse with those who have passed on, and heal. Yes, this is all part of the universe, and the universe is all part of the Divine.

Remember that line in the Desiderata ode? It goes:

> You are a child of the Universe,
> No less than the trees and the stars;
> You have a right to be here.
> And whether or not it is clear to you,
> No doubt the Universe is unfolding as
> it should.

That little verse says so much, don't you think? And it should do so, as it is telling you the origins of humanity and its path in the stars.

Learn what you need to learn, believe in yourself, and love yourself and others. Take kindly to the years that pass over you as it shows the growing perfection within you. Be gentle with yourself also, for though you have many gifts, humanity is very fragile in your world.

Let it be so and let the Divine's love be with you. I shall leave you now to contemplate my words.

Bless you!

Raphael

The Journal: Year 2014

January 3, 2014

Channelled Message

There is a little of a lot within us. What is meant of that is that there are a lot of wonderful and amazing things out in this universe. We all have a little of that within us. As you look out into the depths of space and to the stars, you are looking deep within yourself.

Remember that phrase: As above, so below; as below, so above. It is said to be Wiccan, but it can be said of spiritualism.

As the archangels surround our world with their love, they are also with us inside. There is a little part of us that is within the archangels, just as there is a little part of them that is within us. It makes for very loving connections and strong bonds.

Once you have contacted an archangel, your life is changed for the better. This is because it is an eye-opening experience for humans. The archangels are powerful, omnipresent, and loving. They are part of the Divine. We too are part of the Divine—hence that link between the angels and us. This is a link that will never die, and it is to be treasured forever. It is a link that is so powerful and yet so gentle. The Archangels are magnificent and loving. They are a part of us in energies, as we are part of them.

The angels live to help and assist us. We live to grow and become the guardians the angels want us to be. Yes, guardians of this world and of other worlds. As we grow in our minds and world, we will become the ascended. The previous ascended masters will go further in their path to be part of the Divine plan. And in turn, we too will follow them in time. This is just a small portion of what goes on in your universe. We all grow and move ahead. Nothing ever ends or stops—nothing!

Go forward in peace and let yourself know that it is all part of the Divine's plan. Each step you take makes you grow spiritually—hence the reason why we often say, "Please believe in yourself." After all, within you all is a little part of the Divine. In believing in yourself, you are saying you believe in the Divine.

You understand?

I shall leave you now to contemplate my words. This has made some of you think. That is good, for what you see within your mind's eye is also a revealing small part of the big truth: the Divine's plan. I believe you are all ready for the first steps.

My blessings upon you all.

(Name not understood, as it was starting to fade out due to an energy surge. It sounded like Asariel or similar.)

***

I did a quick private set of questions which were neatly fielded off. I then felt a strong burst of energy surge through me after this, which nearly made me pass out. I called out to Metatron as it was happening, and for the first time, I heard Metatron speak to me. "You are growing." Metatron only contacts me when he thinks I need to grow. I suspect he triggers the growth process.

Right now, the energy has eased off, but my head feels light, and there seems to be a band of energy wrapped around it. It's not painful but feels odd. Swirls of energy are running around me. I must say my headache, which I have had all day, is gone, and my feeling of depression that had been building is also gone. I believe my energy levels, which were down, have now been replaced.

***

January 5, 2014

Be prepared to get an earful. Here's a message from Michael.

Be well and listen up, as my voice would say.

This is a time of intense energies. There are things going on in your world that are not good but are of the forces of negativity. There are wars and famine, and some of those humans who have been put in a place of responsibility are not helping in sorting this problem out. This is not good and is worrying for you.

Take heed; they will be held accountable for their actions. They will have to judge themselves, and it will not look good for their own eyes. These people will then have to incarnate again to learn some valuable lessons. Like humility, charity, and above all compassion.

We do not throw people into this hell you all imagine, for there is no such place. The only hells are of your own creation. These hells are what your own guilt has made. The only way to destroy your own hell is to forgive, love, give charity, and take the first steps out of the bad situation you created for yourself.

This is what these people who are in power must learn. They are inadvertently creating their own hell. They will fall victim to their own nightmares. That is not good, but it is inevitable. You humans have a name for it: karma.

Yes, my voice, it is me who is stroking your hands. Thank you for deleting that paragraph. It was for you and you only.

Please, everyone, be patient. Some of those who are doing good things in this life are also suffering from others' judgmental ways. This is their path of learning too. They are learning to follow their own path and to ignore what others say. They are learning strength of Spirit. And to those who are judging others? Did not Jesus say, "Judge not, lest you be also judged"? That's right: it works both ways. In judging others, you are showing others what you are really like. That is a weakness in you. If you have a judgmental opinion on someone, think about it. Investigate why you should feel that way and what earthly reason why you want to feel that way, as it is not good.

Acceptance, love, forgiveness, laughter, harmony, and joy are all parts of perfection.

I say to those who are in places of power and corrupt their positions: Look deep within yourself. Do you like what you see? Learn from your mistakes and correct them. Learn compassion and humility quick, and you will greatly redeem yourselves.

To those who have struggled against such powers: Forgive, learn, and don't let anything break your spirit. This is an opportunity to learn on how power can corrupt and turn people.

To those who judge others and put them down, all you are doing is letting in more of the dark negativity into your soul. This can drag you down to the lower levels of your spirit. Learn to let go, take an interest in something that can help people, learn to laugh, dance, and of course give charity freely without any cost.

I say all this to those who have dealt with turmoil in this world. I say this because I need to. Listen and learn, my friends.

And finally, to those of the light who give themselves to the light willingly, I will give my love and help. You have reached a soul state that saves you from the lower levels. You are more of the light than of the dark, and each incarnation brings you nearer to us. In time you will become ascended.

You have all learned to let go and move on with your lives. You don't need positions of power. You have the power of the light within you.

Yes, please grow into the soul flowers you are.

My voice, I hear you. I agree there is much to be said, yet it must not be said because time is not ready for it. Relax and leave your worries behind. No, I will not tell you about a certain incident in your near future. That is for you to find out, but you won't have to wait long. Either way, your work with us is not done and will never be done. We all love you, and we promise that you will always be our voice.

All in all, we have said this before, and we will say this again. Believe in yourself, believe in us, and believe in the Divine.

Thank you. I shall leave you now.

Michael

***

January 8, 2014

A brief message from Archangel Michael.

The Divine said, "Let there be light," and during this all the necessary ingredients to make you were ready. The light is part of you, and you are part of the light. Believe in you, and you will believe in the light. Grow with this knowledge and grow with it.

Forever walk towards the light, and the light within you will grow stronger.

Hold your head high up with confidence and joy.

You are perfect as you are. You are beautiful. You are part of the Divine.

Be joyful and be blessed.

Michael

***

January 9, 2014

A message from Archangel Jophiel.

Well, it's that time again. Time for reflection. Time for reviewing the good times. Time for reviewing the incidents that have made memories for you. Yes, even time to consider your own selves. This is a time where you need to become involved with the light because it sure is going to get involved with you. Don't fight it because its aim is to empower you. Bring on the stars, the glitter, and the many sparkles. Celebrate the new you as you embrace the light.

Gently love those who surround you. Whether that person is a close friend or an enemy to you, love knows no bounds. It is all-encompassing. Even love your cat or dog. In fact, all animals and plants deserve your love. Give it freely, and it will be returned thricefold.

Ah, yes, it is a very monumental time for you all. Things are happening all over your world. I'm not talking about the "big freeze," as some of you call it. I'm talking about the changes on a spiritual level. Quite a few of you have grown far. But remember, such big steps will take you far, and you must not forget those who are just coming into their gifts at a lower level. Your job is to teach those beginners to rise too. The more you bring into the light, the greater the love you will receive. Each one of you that joins with the light is a force for the light. This force will be mightier than any army and can change the world for the better; this can be done by manifestation and thought.

You can do this, and you will. We will help you to grow and change.

You are our star children.

We will bless you.

We will welcome you.

I thank you all for hearing my words.

Jophiel

***

January 25, 2014

A message from Archangel Raphael.

Welcome, all.

How are you all keeping now? All ready for your weekend? I hope so!

Your weekend is your rest and recuperation from your busy week. Your body needs it, and you must look after your selves. This is so with your spirit guides; they too need rest if they've been busy. During times of your work or activity during the week, your guides are constantly monitoring, healing, energizing, and directing you. When you rest, they rest. A weekend is a time when they can slow down with you. Healing is still done but at a slower and deeper level. During that break, you inwardly are helping to heal yourselves.

Now, isn't that wondrous?

Yes, you need your rest to help you heal yourselves from within. Your soul also heals during that time. Now, let me help you with all that. I am Raphael, and I'm going to give you a few tips on healing.

When meditating, surround yourself with the white light and breathe it into yourself.

Then imagine my emerald green light mixing with the white light.

Now breathe in both colours into yourself.

Imagine the combined light permeating throughout your body and saturating each living cell within you.

Keep this breathing in the light for around fifteen minutes of your time.

Call upon me.

During this time, my healing light will work through you, healing you. I will guide the light to the parts that need it the most. Some of you may even feel my presence or my touch. That is good. Relax when that happens, for it means that I am around and helping. So don't fear my touch, for I will never harm you, but I will heal and love you.

If there is an illness that I appeared to have ignored, don't worry, I know it's there, and I have eased it a bit for you. If I were to heal you of this illness suddenly, your body would go into shock. Hence it will be a gradual process. Some others may think that I have ignored their ills. Not so. Those types of illness are those of the teaching type. You were destined to have that illness to learn from them. Once learned, you will recover for your next lesson.

All will take time; all will take your inner strength. All will take your love and your belief in yourself.

Too fast is worse than too slow as all things will come right at the right time: no sooner, no later.

I bid you well. Yes, that pun was deliberate.

Raphael

***

January 26, 2014

This happened a few days ago.

I was sitting and working at my computer on Facebook, as usual. I felt a presence and something like a hand rest on my head. Now, this is normally an indicator that my guides or an angel want to talk to me.

I tuned in, as one does, and soon sensed the presence of my teacher, Gabriel. He stood behind me but did not say anything. He smiled at my noticing him and greeting him, but he remained silent.

It was then I realised that this was a moment where words weren't needed, and I asked if it was so. He smiled and nodded. I relaxed in his presence and let his loving energy soothe me. Smiling, I decided to stretch my arms out and stretch them upwards. I felt Gabriel's hands gently take my hands and hold them in place. He ran his hands over my forearms. I felt the soothing energy. Soon I had to put my hands down, and he put his hand back on my head.

Not long after that, he left.

Since then, I'm now channelling much easier. It's now obvious I've been given a boost. I consider Gabriel my teacher and a best friend or big brother to me.

***

January 27, 2014

A Message from Archangel Azrael.

Welcome!

Let us talk about your dreams. I'm not talking about those you have at night, but daydreams. They are important to us because they let us know what you want in life.

You dream of a beautiful holiday? Well, then, put pictures of the place you want to go to on a corkboard or on the fridge with your magnets. Have plenty of these pictures and take time throughout the day to look at them and dream of being there.

The more often you do this, the better it is.

Envision the details also, such as paying for the trip, receiving your flight tickets, packing and boarding your flight, and so on. Such details give us the blueprint of what you want to happen. This is called manifesting.

Also, tell us what you want. Say it out loud; we hear you and always will. We hear everything. We cannot turn our backs to you, and we don't want to. Call upon us, tell us, show us your dreams, and share the love. Yes, share the love. We love you, and when you give us love, it is like a thank-you to us. Our love is unconditional, and we do like to receive love too. Just like you. The more you share love, the more love you will receive—karma at its finest.

Wonderful people, we are waiting, but at the same time we are very active. We are busy trying to heal, grow, comfort, and protect; loving; speaking; and even spreading the Divine's love. Yet we are doing a lot more than this. Despite how busy we are, we have all the time in the world to hear you. It's because time has no meaning here. It's all part of oneness.

Clear as mud, I know! But you will understand when you cross over to us.

Do you believe in yourself? If so, then this manifesting we were talking about will be easy. You are all more than what you think yourselves as. Much, much more! Throw away those niggling self-doubts and open yourself to the real you! The real you are confident, joyful, intelligent, open, and above all loving! Show the world the real you!

Once you have grown into the real you, you will find that life will get a lot easier. Good things will happen to you. Obstacles in your way will suddenly become nothing. Don't let others try to smother the real you. They're jealous. They have yet to discover their own selves, and they won't notice for a while because they are younger souls. But in time and in future incarnations, they will open themselves to the wonderful power of the Divine self. Yes! Some of you are starting to realise that the real you are your Divine self. It is part of your spiritual growth. Your higher self is at the pinnacle of your own growth and is watching over you.

Be well, my loves, and let my words give you comfort.

I am Azrael, and I did say I would be back.

Azrael

***

January 31, 2014

A message from Archangel Chamuel.

Welcome, my beloved ones.

Remember that song from a while back, "What Is Love?" Well, that is what I'm going to talk about.

What is love?
Love is when all things good and wonderful reach into your soul and join.
Love is the stars in the sky.
Love is the Divine who watches us all.
Love is within us all.
Yes, love is you!

We all need love, we all can give love, and we all can receive love. We all can embody love; just look in the mirror. You are love! So love yourself as you would love others, and love others as you would love yourself. As you do this, the aspect of your world will begin to change. You will find you will experience many enlightening moments.

Is it too hard to ask? Not at all!

After all, you were all made from love with love. Therefore, you are the embodiment of love. We too can feel love, and we give it freely. So must you. Give your love freely and be amazed at what you get back.

You will find yourself receiving more and more love. Things will link into place; miracles will happen. The reason why? Because in giving others your love, you have received love from the Divine. The Divine helps those that receive that love.

There will be some who say it's all hormones and chemicals from the body. Sure it is, but that feeling is for real. Without those chemicals and such, we'd have nothing to work with, and you would be as cold as stone in your hearts. That's not a good thing. Come on and let love be your shining light in a dark place. Let yourself be the bringer of that shining light and shine your love for us all. You can move mountains with love. You can cure a lot of illness with love.

Love is the most powerful thing in the world because it is a gift from the Divine. Be love and be receiving of love. I love you, and that is wonderful.

I shall leave you with my words to read.

I thank you all.

Chamuel

***

February 3, 2014

As I sat down, I felt a hand firmly on my head. This is an indication that an angel or a guide wants to speak to me. I tuned in and got this message.

> Well, we meet you all again. What a wonderful day it has been. A day of promise and a day of blessed love. Some of you may not think this at this moment but reflect on that day. Did you see the beautiful dawn? Hear a singing bird? Or even hear a child's laughter? These are the wondrous things I am thinking of. The wonders of nature are many and all there for you to see. Your world is a jewel in the cosmos. Treasure her wonders.
>
> Raise your love to the sky and open your hands to receive love back. Open your hearts to let that love flow through it and embrace it from within. It is healing, isn't it? And you have free and ready access to it.
>
> Now reflect again on your day. It was a lovely day indeed. You now remember things that you had missed out on but in fact were in front of your eyes. Beautiful things. They were missed out because you were too busy rushing around doing things. Have you stopped to look at a simple flower? That flower is not so simple when you think of it. It has many complexities, including life. Take time to slow down and observe the beauties that your world contains.

Take a walk during idle moments and treasure such life that nature brings. As you walk among nature, you will become energized, and it helps to ground you. Nature is loving and forgiving; you are her children as well as our students.

We will teach you about the wonders of nature, the wonders of the cosmos, and the wonders of our realm. Just open your hearts to the beauty of the Divine love, the love that is ours, the love that the Divine has for us all.

Yes, as I said earlier, send some back to the Divine and us in return. For in causing this exchange, our bond with each other will strengthen.

Be at peace with yourselves on this. After all, it is pure love and of the light. Be free with this love, and let it pour over you like the golden light of the sun. Absorb this golden light and bathe in it. Let it filter through to your very essence. Bask in its exhilarating warmth. This is one of our many gifts to you. A gift that the Divine has told us to share with you. Be well in heart, mind, and spirit, for they are all one.

I bless you all with my love and treasure you.

Michael

After this, I felt the hand press more firmly and an arm across my shoulders. They're still there while I type this.

***

February 5, 2014

A message from Uriel.

> Now is the time of wonder, of peace, and of light. Now is your time to belong with such wonders. Don't hold back; let it go through your very soul. Let it flow with your heart light blazing. Let it show the world that you are golden. You are of the light.
>
> You are beautiful people, my lightworkers. You are, and don't let any others say otherwise. You are special. You are my wondrous joy.
>
> Do not hesitate to spread your wings of light and enfold others with them, just like my friends enfold you with their light. This is so. You should relax in our love. Be joyful and at peace in our light. We are your friends, and you are ours. We have much to offer you, and some of those offers are of love.
>
> As you grow into your abilities, you are growing inside and out. As you do this, others will notice the changes in you. You appear to be more relaxed and happier, and you laugh more. That is our doing. You deserve such inner peace.
>
> We too love to laugh and share our joy. As you laugh at the antics of a kitten, we laugh with you. It's all good and of the light. Such joy heightens your vibrations and makes you closer to us. So step

up, step out, and let it all hang out. Or as the phrase I once heard some time ago, "Chill out!" You are the future of your world and the future of your incarnations. What you do now will help you in your next incarnations. Slacken now, and you will be brought back at the same level repeatedly until you learn.

Learn now and embrace the love the light gives you. Show the world you are a lightworker, and you will advance in any next incarnations. When you cannot advance anymore because you have learnt all you can, you will ascend. Yes, that's right. Did you know what ascendancy means to you? It means that you will have no need of your physical form. You will be like us: powerful, gentle, loving, and our greatest friends.

This is the future we hope for you all. For you are our land-based friends, and we want you to grow into the light. You will share our adventures, our love, and our lives. You will be our beloved light friends. That is wondrous, for that is the light and the Divine's vision for you, my star children. Be glad, for there is no greater honour.

I bid you farewell for now.

Blessed be.

Uriel

***

February 9, 2014

An interesting moment happened just now. I had been feeling depressed for no reason. I felt tiredness was only a partial cause, so I knew what to do. I called upon Michael to cut links of any negative energies that were pulling me down. Soon I felt a hand on one side of my head, and another hand gently lay on the other side. Then I felt the presence of Michael.

His words to me after I greeted him were, "All done!" and, "Believe in yourself." We had a quick chat for a few minutes, and then he left with a parting "Go for it!"

Right now, I don't feel down in the gob anymore. I am now feeling fine. Yep! I really love the archangels. We are friends indeed.

Another thing: yesterday, I was in a bookshop and found my feet meandering to a shelf of books. There on the shelf was this single book: *The Miracles of Archangel Gabriel* by Doreen Virtue. I asked Gabriel if this book was for me. It was confirmed.

Later that night, I read through the book. I soon came across the chapter about Gabriel and writers. That was when it clicked with me why I was told to get the book. I asked, and it was confirmed. I checked further in the chapter and noticed that a journal was to be kept, as well as other relevant notes. I was already unwittingly doing that. I asked Gabriel this, and it was again confirmed that I would be required to do this. I had already been keeping notes. I was also told that there was still a long way to go on this path, but I'm on schedule. It also appears that they all want to talk more with me, and I was to add my artwork to the journal. Damn! I haven't dated that stuff.

Erk!

***

February 16, 2014

A new message from Archangel Chamuel.

Welcome, my beloved ones. Welcome!

Did you all enjoy your day of love? I believe quite a few of you had some great moments during this, but please remember there is more to love than just gifts and romance.

Love is universal, and it surrounds everyone, including those who have no partner to share it with. Love comes from pets, family, and us! We give it all to you, and you share it around to others. Even spare some for yourself. Aren't we all deserving of this love? Hmm? Yes, you are, including your pets, your family, and even a simple potted plant. They are all created by love, with love, and for love. So don't hold yourselves back from this feeling. It is there for all of you, and there is no shortage of it either.

The origins of all this love? Well, it's all from the Divine. Accept that just as much as the Divine accepts you.

Now, let us speak of other things.

Some of you are feeling the changes happenings around you—the feelings of depression, pain, headaches, and exhaustion. This is caused by changes that are happening right now, the changes that will bring your world into a new phase. During this time, be patient with yourself and others. Yes, it is going to affect everyone. Quite a few of you are starting to realise what is happening already. The best way to cope with it is meditation. This will help you gain inner peace, calm, and control. This method will ease the feelings and effects of such a massive change. Let yourself bathe in the golden light of the Divine. This too is free for all to access. Just meditate and visualise yourself surrounded in this golden light. Let it absorb into you at the cellular level. It will help you to focus, cleanse and reach peace. This golden light is the Divine's love that is gifted to you all.

I'll let you be part of love, be in love, and be with love.

I bid you all goodbye for now.

Chamuel

At the end of this message, I felt a hand go across my shoulders and then down to my left hand.

***

February 16, 2014

I had an interesting moment with Gabriel this morning. He gave me the usual indicator that he wanted to chat. I let him into my head, but he didn't talk. I tuned out a bit, and he began to show me images of a being who had dark silver eyes and dark silver hair; there was friendship in those eyes. It seems that this one will get in contact with me soon and work together. I felt Gabriel was doing something in my head.

Soon after that, he began to chat with me. Basically, he told me that he had done some alterations in my ability, and I'd know what they were soon enough. I should not worry and should go forward. He did something to my ability again that had my mind and body doing spasms; my head seemed to rock forwards and back. This was a massive surge of energy. He separated his consciousness from me, stroked my cheek, wished me well, and then left.

Should be interesting things happening soon.

***

February 18, 2014

This was done on a Facebook page for a site I now no longer run.

A Message from AA Gabriel, My Teacher:

I welcome you all!

We have much information to exchange and a lot to share, including the sharing of love, light, and friendship. I too have those to share with you all, and I am willing to do so. Just ask and ask with love in your hearts. This is one offer that is ready and waiting for you all.

Now, who's first?

Let's speak of other things. Of sailing ships and sealing wax, of cabbages and kings. Ah, some of you are already recognising what book that came from. I am talking about a lovely book so full of innocence, imagination, and joy. It is all about a little girl who dreams and lives her dreams.

That is what I want to talk to you about.

How many of you are living your dream? Not many, I noticed. Well, what is stopping you from doing that? Some say lack of cash; others say they don't have the time. There are so many excuses being made by you; you're holding yourself back. Live your dreams.

Live them, and the rest of your dreams will follow through. Lack of cash? I don't think so. If you really wanted that cash, you would manifest it, visualise gaining it. All you need to do is ask us.

But then again, the real dream is with us; we will share your dream of perfection. A dream can become a reality if you want it to be real. That is why you have imaginations, aspirations, and inspiration. They are there to help you move forward and live that dream.

It is only in your world that you are taught as a child to smother your dream and get a career to pay your way. It's not necessary! Living that dream will make you so happy that your vibrations will increase greatly. This is a big step towards perfection, so don't rubbish it.

It is then you realise that your material wants aren't all that important. Your needs can be met by us, but your inner light and soul are the most important thing in this world and our world, for they are the very embodiment of the Divine within you, and it is this soul that makes you perfect. Giving yourself joy and laughter makes the Divine feel your joy. The Divine treasures that.

Is it not beautiful? Yes, it is! It is as beautiful as you are, my lightworkers. You are all beautiful in our eyes. Let us leave this message as a thought for you.

Emrayel has just said to me, "Think of it like butter: spread it around." I agree! Spread my words around like the honey they are. Yes, Em, I think honey is a better word than butter.

I bid you all well.

Gabriel

***

March 6, 2014

Interesting things are happening here. My clairvoyance has taken off to new heights, I've got three portraits, and my meditations have been amazing. I had felt a need for meditation and found myself sinking rapidly into it. In it, I found myself looking at a woman in her late thirties with brown hair, puce and plum veil, and matching dress. She was sitting at an old Victorian desk.

I found myself saying that I was an angel channel. She darted out of her chair at high speed, went behind me, and gently rested her hand on the left side of my head. I roused up.

Curious, I asked Gabriel about this. He didn't say anything, but I felt him near me. He didn't place his hand on my head like he usually does if he wants to chat. I went under a trance state and invited him into my head if he wanted to. He entered my head. I asked him who the woman was, and he replied Mary or Marie. He went silent. I found myself going deeper into the trance and "saw" Gabriel beside me. It turned out that my clairvoyance has been boosted more. He showed me some pictures via thought.

I looked towards my left and saw Michael watching me, gently smiling. I greeted him, and his smile broadened into a wide grin.

I began to come out of my meditation.

Ten minutes later, I felt Gabriel's hand on my head, indicating he wanted to talk. Again I went into a trance mode. I got the images of humanity in various roles of parents, laughter, working, and sleeping. I even saw one man with dark hair but electric blue eyes (indicating he was not human) lie down on his side in front of me and watch me. He even appeared relaxed.

These visions stopped and were replaced with darker images of pain, poverty, hatred, and negativity. I heard Gabriel say to me, "There are no second choices."

I knew what he meant. It was time for me to choose my path: the path to darkness and sorrow, or the path to the light and joy. I roused out of my trance and said, "I choose the path of light. I choose the path to divinity. I choose the path that is perfection and harmony. I choose the path of light." I felt an enormous rush of emotions and a feeling something had shifted within me. I had asked if I had chosen wisely and was told I had.

Twenty minutes ago, I found myself slipping into a light trance and saw Michael stretch forward. With a cheeky grin on his face, he poked me in the stomach. My response? I stuck out my tongue at him. I felt the chuckling.

It now appears I can "see" the angels. Even my own guardian angels have shown themselves to me. This is getting more and more common.

This is the woman whom I saw at the desk.

***

March 11, 2014

Lately, I've been feeling surrounded by love and an inner peace growing within. Many people have started to comment that I am appearing to be more relaxed, laughing more, and happier. I suspect a certain bunch of angels are the culprit. I had been told by another angel channel that an archangel was surrounding me with their wings.

For the last couple of nights, I have had an angel come to visit me, helping to keep me calm and patient during a stressful moment. I asked her name, and she said Abigail. Her name was then confirmed within these two days repeatedly by appearing in books, notes, and other media. I found out that she was sent to me by Michael, who is protective of me.

I've just asked Gabriel, and he said Abigail would come back every time I'm in that stressful situation (the stressful situation is a telephone switchboard), and because I get on with her.

***

March 12, 2014

A new message from an archangel who has been nagging at me to pass his message on, but I was unable to do so because my PC had broken down on me.

Hear my words, hear them well.

I come to you to say that you are all beautiful and that beauty is all perfect in the eyes of the Divine. Yes, you! I'm talking to all of you.

Don't hide your inner beauty from others. Don't let others take that beauty from you. Stand tall, blossom like the very rose of light you are, and show off your inner beauty. That is what the Divine has given you, and you are permitted—no, encouraged to show it off.

Now, don't you feel good about yourself?

Yes, and in doing so, your vibrations have risen to a higher level, a level that your guardian angels and guides can work with you, as it is part of your growth and inner healing.

Grow my flowers of golden light. Grow and grow tall. Let it be so.

Already a few of you are feeling the love that is starting to surround you as you blossom forth. That love is from us all. As you raise your vibrations, you will feel our love more clearly. That is meant to be, just as is your growth in the light. Such is the Divine's flowers of golden light, and they are you.

Well done! Some of you have reached that stage long before you read this message, and I see them all.

You are all welcome in our eyes and the Divine's eyes. We all love you, even those who haven't advanced enough to raise their levels. We love you too and will watch over you patiently until you begin to blossom forth.

You too are a flower bud in a field of golden blossoms. You just need the right moment to open and show your hidden inner beauty.

Bless you all, and I will repeat that again many times in your lives here in your world. Bless you all again.

I am Jophiel, I am joy, and I am your angel of happiness.

Call on me if you ever feel you are falling into the depths of unhappiness. I will come to you with love and light. I will lighten your load upon your heart. I do this because I can, and I will do this because I love you all.

I am Jophiel, and I can do this for you.

Blessed be to you all, my friends.

Jophiel

Right now, he's saying, "I don't nag … I'm just persistent," and he is laughing.

***

March 12, 2014

Some time ago during a meditation session, I saw a face, and that face had friendship in its eyes, but something in me was not so sure. I asked Gabriel, and he told me that this was Abaddon. Gabriel also told me that I could draw his picture. Uriel added that I was protected, and that Abaddon would never be allowed near me.

They both insisted that I draw the face. Their reason? "Draw the picture for from memory, for your memory."

It seems that in drawing Abaddon, I was to remember the face, and in doing so, maybe I'd know whom to avoid. Know thy enemy? Hmm! Anyways, I've drawn Abaddon, and I confess his pose reminds me of a wannabe porn star!

***

March 19, 2014

A message from a healing angel with whom I work.

> Be yourself!
>
> Don't follow in another's shadow, or you will lose your own. You have your own shadow, and it belongs to you only. Your own shadow tells you that you are fully in the light. Follow your light, and your shadow will follow you. Let others follow your light but be careful not to cover them with your shadow. For they have their own light to follow, not yours. Your light is for you only. Don't let others force you into their shadows, for their path is not yours. Back away and go into your own light space and grow.
>
> Meriel

***

March 21, 2014

A message from an angel I have never spoken to before, Amariel. She's one of the angels of love.

It's over now. The time for trouble and upsets is over. Now is the time for you to grow and reach for the light of the Divine. You are asking, "What is over?" I'll tell you! Your struggle to reach the light is what is over, for you have all managed to reach it. And now you can relax, laugh, and even sing your joy. We all like it when you are happy with yourselves. For it means you have found peace and love inside you. That is what makes you fantastic!

So now you can lead others less advanced onto their new path of enlightenment. Show them the light and let them bathe in it. For that is what your tasks are: to bring more people into the light. Now that is a job well worth doing and doing well. If you wonder how you can do this job? Simple! All you must do is show your follower your love for them and for everyone. Show them your love for the Divine and us. All in all, you could say just show your Divine love.

And it feels wonderful, doesn't it?

Now as you love others, you will find that our love for you will grow. Let it be so and love it. This is all part of growing and developing, as you grow, so does your inner light, your love, and your spirituality. It's all part and parcel of enlightenment, you know. It's all worth it. I can guarantee that.

Don't ever think no one loves you, or that you are alone in this. You will never be alone while there are angels. For we angels love you all unconditionally and when you advance in your enlightenment, you will also love all unconditionally. Just like us.

Love is wonderful.
Love is divine.
Love is everywhere.
Love is thine.

Enjoy your new-found Divine love and spread it wherever you go. You'll be surprised at how many will return it, even strangers.

Be with God, no matter how you conceive God to be. For God and the Divine are one. You and the Divine are one. You and we angels are one.

Bless you and grow in peace, love, and enlightenment.

Amariel

***

March 22, 2014

A message from another archangel that I have occasionally spoken to, yet I have always seen him in the background, watching. He only comes to me when he thinks my abilities are ready to go a notch higher.

Right now, as I sit here typing, I feel as if a finger is poking me in the third eye. There is pressure and yet no pain, just pressure.

> Let go, beloved. Let go.
>
> You are all on a journey to the light. Light of such purity and grace that it overwhelms you with its Divine love. This light is your destination when you have learnt all you have learnt. This is called oneness.
>
> As you are all part of that light, that light is all part of you. As you reach your final destination, you become that light in all of its radiant beauty. Some of you, who are more advanced in spirituality, will become one with us in our ranks. Some others will become ascended masters, and yet others will become guardians or gatekeepers to new worlds.
>
> As you see, you all have a task to perform when the time comes, and no one will be forgotten. Beloved ones, never lose your sense of direction and fall from the path. Always look to the Divine's light, and you

will never be left behind or stray. For this is your destiny. Yes, all of you!

Now, many times I have watched some of you try to walk the path of light and yet fall by the wayside. Did any of you lightworkers give up? No! You persevered and climbed back on, and you made that path your own. You are becoming near your target, and the light within you is getting stronger. The path is hard, but it is hard for a reason. It is hard so to strengthen your will and your heart. The more you let the Divine's light enter your heart, the easier the path will become. And most of all, do not ever lose your sense of humour. We find your laughter is a joy to us, and it brings so much pleasure to us all.

It is all worth it in the end, I assure you. You will not be disappointed. In fact, quite a lot of you will rather enjoy it. Yes, it is indeed a goal to aim for.

Now, let me help you there by this simple exercise. You know the techniques of meditation and breathing.

When you go into this meditative state, visualise being surrounded by a giant golden orb of light.

As you breathe, breathe in this golden light until it is absorbed to the atomic level in your body.

This will help you absorb more of this Divine light, and you can take as much of it as you want. You can even meditate in this light as often as you like. It is yours to take in, to enjoy.

This light is healing, is cleansing, and raises your vibration level. You can call upon us during this time for any healing, love or just to visualise. Your guides find it easier to talk to you during this time, and you will find it easier to talk to them and us.

I shall leave you with your thoughts and this message.

Metatron

***

March 27, 2014

Here's a picture of one of my guides, which I did this morning. He wouldn't give me a name because he said I didn't need to know. But he has agreed to let me call him Mac to save confusion. He's a Scots Highlander, is very protective of me, and says he is my strength. He had quite an earthy sense of humour.

***

April 2, 2014

Just came back from a group session. When the healing part was done, I was told by another medium that during the healing session, she could see folded wings on my back.

I was learning to heal from Meriel (a healing angel) at that time, and so I can only assume she saw Meriel's presence.

(In a few years' time, I would learn the real reason, which was quite an eye-opener and shook me mentally.)

***

April 2, 2014

A message from an angel who wanted me to pass its message on last night, but I was too exhausted. We agreed that I'd do this message tonight. Now, I've never spoken with this angel before, but I get the impression that it does not mince words and is rather forthright to the point of blunt in manner. I shall introduce you to the angel Jadziel.

> I see too many people giving their power away to others. Too many allow themselves to be subjugated and for what? For no purpose at all but to feed power to the one who is controlling them. Well, stop it! You are not that person's power source. You are not under others' control. You are never meant to be. That is not your purpose.
>
> Your purpose is to grow into the light with your head high, and with a heart of love. That is your ultimate power! The power of "I AM!" Look into a mirror, stare at yourself in the eyes, say "I AM" loudly, and keep on repeating this. It is very powerful, and it gives you strength when others try to take your power. These are words of confirmation, strengthening of will and it is also the Divine's own words of being. "I AM" is a word of power.
>
> Once you start to believe in yourself as "I AM", you start to grow into the light, like the very seed that has burst out a single leaf. One leaf at a time, you will grow stronger. Just like the acorn that sprouts and grows into an oak tree. You say, "I AM," and you

are at the same time acknowledging the fact that you are powerful, you are strong, and you are beautiful. That word is your self-accepting all these and more. It also means that you are accepting the Divine into your heart.

The result? You will make those words a big part of you, a part that is stronger than any steel rod. Stronger than anything in your world. The words will make you believe in yourself and feel part of the Divine. These are words that are more than hope; they are words of love.

Hmm, beautiful.

Let it be so. And now another word.

Some people need to look at the world around them. See flora and fauna in its abundance; they too are part of you. They are part of your soul. Take care of how you treat your world, because in abusing or destroying parts of it, you in turn are destroying part of your ultimate parent and parts of your spirit. Not good, is it? Show the world your love and care for the creatures that walk upon it. Take pleasure in each plant that sprouts on it, big or small. As I said, they're part of you.

I tell it like it is.

Well, my beautiful friends. With these words, I bid you all a temporary farewell. I am Jadziel, and I know only a few know me. I generally keep in the background. But those who do know me know I don't hold back. I say my words with love, for I don't want you to make things worse for yourself.

Love your world, and the world will love you back.

This will help towards your spiritual growth.

Jadziel

***

April 11, 2014

A message from my teacher, Archangel Gabriel.

> Listen, my friends: things are starting to happen. Good things! Wonderful things! And they are all for you.
>
> Do you yearn for a new job? A job that is more pleasant and pays better? Ask! Say that you want a job that will appreciate you more. Simple as that! Don't say, "I wish I had a better job," as that means nothing more to us than an idle wish. Say you *want*, not *wish*.
>
> Now you understand.
>
> You need a love partner? Same thing. Don't wish—tell us what you want. It's all in the wording. And that is the most meaningful way of getting our attention: the wording. Remove *wish* and replace it with *want*.
>
> Simple as that.
>
> Now, about those wonderful things that are happening. Be prepared for an experience of a lifetime. Energy is starting to peak, and soon you will receive your gifts. In order to receive these gifts, open your heart, your mind, and your hands to them and to us. We want to give you these gifts, but only

if you ask for them. Now, that is very important because we cannot force you into this. You must take the first steps.

Growth is one of these gifts, love is another, and above all the Divine consciousness is the biggest of all. The Divine has given this gift of all-encompassing love. It's yours to take, all yours.

Believe me when I said these are wonderful gifts, for none can resist being loved. No matter who they are, they all need it, and no one is immune to it. So why fight it?

Beloved ones, rest assured that we will never pass over anyone who wants this gift; all will receive, and we will make sure of that. For you to receive these gifts, meditation is a wonderful way to prepare yourself because it does help us a lot by making it easier. Please don't close yourself off and run away. You'll miss out! Open, my dearest ones. Open!

Now for something completely different.

Has anyone put you down and denigrated you? If so, they're the ones who need your sympathy the most. For in attacking they are hiding their own fears and pain. Don't attack back, but instead show them love and care. Keep on giving that love, and soon the cracks in their hard façade will open, and their real selves will show: loving, emotional, caring, and curious. No one is an island; no one is born cruel. You merely have withdrawn from them.

Show kindness to someone who needs it.
Show love to someone who wants it.

Show compassion for those who are hurting within.

And do it all in the name of the Divine. We will help you with this if you ask us. We will never leave you.

Be well, dearest ones. Be true and be love. I shall leave you now with those thoughts and hope you make the right decisions.

I thank you!

Gabriel

***

April 16, 2014

A message from an archangel I've never met or spoken to before: Sandalphon. The message was entirely by telepathy.

> Now is the time for you to go forward. All of you! Not just one. All of you! The time is right and ready. The time is now open for all of you. Will you take the first steps? Will you? Yes, some will, but some won't. Those who won't have their doubts and fears and are letting those control them. Let go of those fears and doubts, they serve no practical purpose in this, as we will never let anything harm you.
>
> Please throw away anything that may hold you back from your first step in evolution. These hindrances are again the doubts and fears, also the negative feelings of anger and hate. Let go of these, in fact, throw them away. You don't need them as you are walking your first steps towards love! Love in its purest form: The Divine! Release those hindrances from your heart and accept the Divine's love to replace those newly opened spaces.
>
> My love and the Divine's love are one, and we are all one in this world and in others. We are love. Let this be so, and never let it be anything else. This is perfection. No matter where you are or where you have come from, you came from love, and you will be forever part of love. This is your past, present, and future. Life is yours for the taking; treasure every

moment and learn from all its aspects, for they are precious, just like you.

Let the precious jewels of love adorn your foreheads. Instead of sapphires, let it be love. Instead of emeralds, let it be love. Instead of diamonds, let this be love also. Let all the other stones be the same: love. I wish you to go forward with this knowledge and know that not all is negative, and that negativity cannot survive when the light of love shines on those harbouring such. It is cleansing, purifying, and so beautiful.

Are you ready to take the first steps? Are you? Then do so, my precious ones. Do so with our blessing and our love. If you find yourself faltering on your path, call on us to help you.

Precious jewels, my precious ones.
You are the stars in the night.
You are the dawning of the light.
Brighter the glittering stones.
Be at peace in the love
That comes outside
And from up above.
Be in the presence of this love.
Grow upwards like the tree.
Go forth up and spread your light
As far as your love light can be free.

Be well and be with my love.

Sandalphon

***

April 21, 2014

A rather humorous message from my teacher, Gabriel, who had me laughing at his gestures and quips.

> Blessed be all the creatures on this world. Blessed be all the plants in this world. Blessed be you: the guardians of this world. You are indeed blessed in more ways than you realise, and in time you will soon find out how much so. We will have great joy in watching your discovery of the gifts the Divine has given you. Your smiles, joy, and amazement give us happiness. That suits us both, I believe. So go ahead. Be happy, be joyful, and live your life to the max. It's all there for you, and all are waiting for you to grab life with both hands and have fun. We will help you too in that; we always enjoy helping others to have a wonderful time. My children, don't hesitate at this moment—just go for it. Just don't forget to look where you step, because you may stumble on a crack or tread on some other person's life.
>
> Have fun and have fun with willing friends or yourself. Your choice, just make sure you do not drag someone in who is unwilling or negative about it. Apart from that, just dance to the music of your life, and no one is pulling your strings. You are free like the very birds in the sky. Open your earth wings and spread them out into your freedom.
>
> Life's like that, you know. All there for everyone to enjoy, just some don't see it. They are blind to their own potential beauty and happiness, and if they see you enjoying your life to the fullest, it may open their eyes to their own promise in life.

Have fun, beloved ones, my precious flowers of life. Have fun and show it.

There is another reason for all your happiness and laughter: it heightens your vibrations, makes it easier for us both to meet and interact with each other. If you are ill but full of happiness, you will heal easier and faster. We can also remove negative bonds much more easily if you are full of life.

Oh, I can go on and on with such descriptions, but it will be interfering with your fun. All I can say is you get my drift. Get out there and get some fun. Go on!

I'm not stopping you this time. Be well, my lovely, fun friends.

Gabriel

***

April 22, 2014

Around midday, I decided to do some meditation. I prepared myself and went into a meditative state. It was easy and quick—too quick. When I slip into this state at that speed, it means that either my guides or the angels have induced it because they need to take me away somewhere. Either way, expect adventures!

Sure enough, as soon as I got to the right stage, I saw myself surrounded by angels of various types. They were smiling and giving the appearance of waiting for me. When they are en masse in front of me, I know they're up to something.

One pointed out an amulet of amber on a gold chain. It was meant to tell me something, but I knew that it was something I'm not to buy; I'd just learn what amber meant to me. *Okay,* I thought. *Note that.*

Another angel then stood in front of me; he looked older than the rest and appeared to be holding a staff. They spoke about me not learning enough, adding that I need to move forward. Okay, I understand. Pull my finger out.

I asked who he was, and he replied, "Does it matter?" I dryly commented that it would stop confusion on my part and that I couldn't go about saying, "Hey, you!" I asked whether we had spoken before (I was starting to get an inkling as to who he was). His reply of "Yes!" clinched it.

"Are you Raziel?" I queried. He smiled, and I felt loving energy confirm my question and then flow through me. He came closer to me, and despite the older face, his hands and body were young. He pointed to somewhere behind him, and I looked up.

I began to soar through a tunnel of light. As I was going through this light, I saw the other angels keeping up with me, watching over me. I soon reached my destination through this tunnel and found myself surrounded by unusual structures made of some strange, glowing white material.

I looked around and saw that Raziel was near me, Gabriel was to my right, and on my left side was Chamuel. They were smiling and giving me loving glances. Raziel indicated that I should look down to my right. As I did so, I saw a massive arena that was surrounded by energy clouds. In the centre was this mass of energy that was so big, no words could describe its size. This energy was surrounded by what appeared to be smaller balls of energy that were linked with lines of energy.

I heard Raziel's voice beside me: "You are looking at Creation."

From the centre of this energy, a massive hand began to form and reached forward to me. It never touched me at all, just hovered above me. I got the feeling that something wonderful had happened. The impression I got from the angels was that this was the Creator: The Divine.

Each archangel that came with me (some were not named here as I didn't see them then) approached, and each appeared to impart something to my subconscious mind. Michael was standing to one side, watching over me, and he appeared relaxed.

Soon it was over, and I found myself going through a long hallway that had pillars running down the sides. At the end was Azrael. I approached him because I always enjoyed his company. But he stepped back, held up a hand, and told me, "It's time to go back." I felt myself returning to my body, and I began to rouse up.

At all times, I felt Gabriel and Chamuel were by my side. Gabriel was to be expected because he is my teacher. The interesting part was Chamuel. I didn't know that he would do this, but it was no surprise as he loves to interact with me. Normally it's Michael who stands by me because he is like a big older brother to me (and often pesters me just as much).

The result: I no longer feel tired out. My energy levels are up. I have a peaceful feeling and one of curiosity. What did happen? Time can only tell.

Gabriel has just said, "And time does."

***

April 24, 2014

A message from someone who has been silent for a while: Chamuel! I did ask for proof that it was him, and he sent me a flow of energy that was such pure love, it nearly rocked me off my seat. Only Chamuel does that to me. He finds it funny that his energy does that to me.

Well, we meet again, and I have seen a few of you have grown more than you have realised. You have grown in ways beyond your own expectations. That is amazing! You are such beautiful people, and you have made me proud of you. I am so pleased with you that you have all earned my blessing, and that I give my blessing freely to all your wonderful people. I bless you all with love and good fortune. Thank you, my friends.

Some have stayed behind, but that's OK. It just means that there is a task for you to do at your current level. You can't advance on until you have done and solved that task. This happens to each one of you at some stage or another. It is normal. Don't feel left out when others have gone ahead. We are still here, and we still watch over you, loving you and helping you.

Let me ask you, Have you all played today? It could be music or just clowning about. Anything playful and fun. If so, well done! Gabriel's words were not in vain. I also enjoy watching you laugh and play. It's so healing, invigorating, and in parts very funny. I've had moments of laughter when I saw some people's antics. Harmless pranks are very good. I particularly liked those.

Ah, you are such wonderful people, and it is such a pleasure to speak with you all. It's been a while I know, and I've never left you. I've always watched over you and waited, but always loving everyone. This time I decided to come forward and share my good news with you all. Yes, with you all!

Look to your neighbour, look at your child, look to your parents, and look at yourself in the mirror. Look in the eyes of the one in front of you and say, "I love you, my friend." And *mean* it. At the same time, visualise pink energy around them or yourself.

That pink energy is love. Feel it, absorb it, and include the person you are facing inside your pink energy. You will be surprised by the results.

Love thy neighbour as you would love thyself. Is it not so written in the Bible? Common sense there, and so wise. If you love yourself unconditionally, then be prepared to offer the open hand of loving friendship with someone near you. When it comes together in perfection and love, the feelings are such a beautiful thing. In such love, there are such riches that are beyond things like jewels and such.

Love is perfect and will empower you.

Love is so true.
Love is so fine.
Love is so pure.

Love is the Divine.

I leave you now with my words of love and joy.

Chamuel

***

April 25, 2014

A little unusual message from an angel I've never met or spoken to before, but it has told me we'll be speaking more often. This is a message from Muriel.

> It's kind of beautiful how the stars do shine.
> High above and glowing with deep love.
> Yours to view and to hold in your hands,
> To place, with joy, into your heart so fine.
>
> This is the gift that is given to you.
> This is what you are born to receive.
> Believe in yourself with love and faith.
> And above all, to yourself be true.
>
> Let the love lie deep within your soul,
> Warming your spirit, and your gifts will unfold.
> It's our gift to give you, so please accept.
> It's a price above all jewels, yet free to all.
>
> A gift of Divine love is yours for the taking.
> Our gift, our blessing, and our happiness for you.
> Please be happy in all your endeavours,
> Whether by fate or in your presence in the making.
>
> Let this be true to all my beloved ones here.
> No one is forgotten; no one will lose.
> You have our love and that of the Divine.
> So accept your happiness true and without fear.

Beloved children, love of our lives, precious souls.
You have a universe ahead in your future.
You have a promise that has been foretold.
You truly have many powerful goals.

Dearest children, you are our tried and true.
You are our children, and we are yours to love.
For we love you in return, and that is the fact.
So lift your spirits up in joy and don't be blue.

Let this little poem be for you all alone,
For no other world can read this; that is true.
For you, my children, are our precious ones.
And I give my blessings, and the poem is done.

Muriel

***

April 27, 2014

During the latter part of the service at the spiritualist church, I "saw" Gabriel standing in the middle of the room and facing the congregation as they were singing. He was conducting the singers with his fingers and singing along. None of the others saw him. He kept flicking glances at me and noticed me trying to smother my laughter. That was when a big, beaming smile crossed his face.

I sent him a message: "You're enjoying yourself, aren't you?"

He came up right next to me and whispered "Yes!" and I felt his laughter.

Gabriel has a great sense of humour.

***

April 28, 2014

A message from Archangel Michael for everyone.

Beautiful people you are. You are beautiful all.

Now, just those few simple words make you all feel special. The reason is that you are *all* special. Yes, all! Now you are feeling even better.

In the eyes of our beloved Divine, you are special. You are special to us as well. We all think you are beautiful. It pleases us that you think of us the same way. This means that we can love each other without conditions. Just so beautiful, isn't it?

Whenever you feel sad or lost, put your hand on your heart and say to yourself, "The Divine says I am beautiful. The angels say I am beautiful. And that is because I am beautiful inside."

Every time you say that to yourself, you will start to believe in it. And once you fully believe that, you will realise that you are surrounded by beauty and that other people will believe you are beautiful and love you for it. It boosts the self-confidence you have. Each time you get that boost, all your insecurities and problems will become less.

We respond to the beauty of your soul, not of your skin. For it is your inner self that is the most important; it strives for perfection and will take you with it, teaching you and learning with you. Your inner self is a part of the Divine. Just like us. We are all part of the Divine, and the Divine works through us all. Each bit we learn in our existence adds knowledge and enables us to help you even better. Win-win, you could say, for both of us. You win by having our attention, love, and help; we win by your love for the Divine and us.

This is the beauty of the inner self. It gives out such unconditional love for you and us.

Stand in front of that mirror and tell yourself that you love the way you are inside and out. Tell yourself that you are also beautiful in all ways. Do this often enough, and in the end, you will start to feel fantastic!

Oh, you are all so lucky. I love you all, and that won't stop. I love your world, and I love your emotional colours. Your auras are like the jewels that glitter on this world of yours. Glitter on, my beloved ones. Glitter on and show your love light.

I leave you now to savour my words.

Michael

***

May 2, 2014

As requested, I'll answer how I started in this lark of angel channelling.

I was at the local spiritualist church at the time as a psychic artist. During this, I tuned into the spirit level to see who my first visitor was. Tuning into spirit level was difficult for me because they seem to be on a different level as to what I can access. It seemed like my mind was wading through deep mud. I couldn't feel any spirit, yet I felt the urge to draw a picture. I got my pad and a pencil and started drawing. The only emotion I felt was anticipation, and it certainly wasn't from me.

As I did my sketch, a beautiful face began to show under my pencil. There was also a message which I had written down. The message I will not write down here because it was a personal message for someone else. Once I reached the end of the message, it was signed off as Raphael.

That is how my first contact with the angels went.

Raphael visited me repeatedly within the next few weeks, and then Gabriel took over my teaching. Gabriel told me that he was to be my mentor, and he trained me for angel channelling. Under his training, I got stronger. I'm still growing here. He told me that this had been my destiny since the beginning and that they had been waiting for the right time for me to wake up.

Gabriel also told me that all mediums could interact with the angels in some way or another, but the angels chose the one whom they will use on a permanent basis and will take over the training. He also told me that Raphael came to me to see if I could receive him yet, because he considered me ready. He did this a few more times, and I received him. It was then that the okay was given to get me trained. Yes, Raphael's visits were the trigger that started the whole process.

If I had known what I was letting myself in for, you wouldn't see me for dust as I shot out the door.

I've just heard Gabriel say, "Hey!" at that, followed by some laughter. I love teasing the angels because they tease me.

How do I see angels?

I rarely see the sparks or flickering lights that others see that signify angels. I don't see angels as shadows either. But I do see them as moving nearly transparent, glowing forms through my third eye and in detail. They don't have wings. I feel intense emotions from them, which are either mainly love or laughter. As for hearing them, it's more like telepathy. The words are placed in my head. I know they aren't my words, because there are phrasings in the language which I would never have thought of.

All in all, every medium reacts or works in different ways. There is no sure-fire routine. We are all different, and we all need different ways of working our skills. I started off as a clairsentient and clairaudient. I'm now clairvoyant with telekinetic abilities.

We all grow, and as we grow, our needs and training will change.

I've just recently learnt that if I wanted to speak to the spirit, I must call the spirit by name now. Great! What if I don't know the name?

***

May 3, 2014

A message from an archangel whom I have only spoken to once before, early last year. Time flies. This is a message from Raguel.

> Beloved ones, you are Divine in your own right. You are beautiful, and you are precious to us all. Open your heart to the blessed Divine and open your eyes.
>
> Yes, both your physical eyes and your spiritual eyes. Open them and look within yourself. You will see so much hidden beauty inside of you—all of it hidden away by your complexities, ego, and negativity.
>
> You must throw away those burdens and let your hidden inner beauty flower forth like the very lilies of the field you are. Blossom, my flowers of love; open your petals of love and show the once was hidden beauty that was within you.
>
> Do this with love, energy, and eagerness. Do it, and in doing so, your world will change for the better.
>
> You are becoming a part of that love that belongs to the Divine. You are also sharing that love. Blossom forth freely. Isn't it wonderful that you can do that, and all with the energy of light running through and around you? I tell you to free yourself from all your burdens and shower your love around.

My lovely friends, you have earned your path of life to the Divine; you have worked hard in your past to get there. You are all taking your first steps on this new path. Rejoice in that; it is because you succeeded in bringing the Divine into your heart.

Yes, it is beautiful.

Embrace that Divine light within you with your own personal energy of love. Love will embrace love. In a short time, it will merge and become one. Yes, one! And it will find its home in you. This one love will power through you, cleansing and rejuvenating you as it is meant to be, and the final step to the Divine will show you as the embodiment of pure love.

Love is very beautiful! Yes, I find it exhilarating. I eagerly wait for that moment when I can call you my kin in spirit.

Your world is shifting into a new phase, and that phase will bring many changes to your world and you. The changes will be massive, but for the better. One of those changes is enlightenment. Another is ascension.

Some are you are already seeing what I am seeing, and that is good! It means that you are nearer to the stage of completion than others. Ah, I could go on and on about how wonderful this is, but I won't! This is your path of discovery and growth. You will soon find out for yourself the wonders you will encounter on your journey.

Beloved ones, I give you all my love, and I shall finish my message. Be well and be of good cheer. Laughter is another form of love, after all.

Love and light,

Raguel

***

May 4, 2014

A familiar hand on my head told me that an angel wanted me to pass on a message. So here is a message from our beloved friend, Archangel Michael.

> Well, we meet again! This is fun!
>
> Do you know that you are what you make yourself to be? You are what you want to be.
>
> You have set limits on yourself which aren't needed.
>
> You have put boundaries on yourself which are not necessary.
>
> You have put the belief of "I can't do this!" set into your mind. This is not wanted.
>
> Remove that doubt and replace it with, "I can do this, and I will!" Then set it in motion. You'll surprise yourself.
>
> You see, all your setbacks and barriers are of your own making. For example, you see a job you would like, but you say, "I haven't got a chance of getting it." That is your barrier there. You have put that boundary around yourself, and you believe in it. This is holding you back. The reality is you do have the chance of getting that job you want. You do have the ability to create your own dreams and live them. You

are the creators of your own future, and you can do anything, *anything,* if you set your mind on it.

Don't ever hold yourself back, or you will end up drowning in self-regret, sadness, and negativity. That is not good for your spirit. You are all made of better things than that. You are made with the love of the Divine and with the power of the universe. You are star children. You are our children.

Believe in yourself, and the rest of the world will believe in you. Show them how to believe in themselves too, and nothing can stop you. You all have the power to be a force for good and the light. The Divine has that intention within you all and has given you this gift. It is a form of free will. It is yours by birth right, and it is yours by Divine right.

Yes! All is as it should, and that is the way it should be. Believe in yourself, my dear ones. We believe in you.

Now it has come to my attention that some of you are hiding your real inner selves from the world. Naughty! That is not how it is meant to be. You are meant to shine out, be a beacon for those needing the light to lead them out of the darkness. Yes, there are some who need you, and they can be around you or just across the road. Be their light, be their beacon, be there!

Shine, my beacons. There is a world out there that needs your light to shine and lead them out from their inner darkness. Step forth, step lightly, and step strongly! Take care to watch your step, though.

You can avoid the cracks of negativity that will try to pull you down by being careful in your footsteps.

Now, how many have heard me? I hear you, and have I heard a lot. I've heard some jokes and have seen people laugh at them. Laugh, my children, for in doing so, you bring yourself joy and love into your life. By the way, I laugh at some of them too. So don't worry about how I feel.

I love you all, and I shall now take leave of my messenger.

Be blessed,

Michael

***

May 8, 2014

A message from an angel I've never spoken to before. This one had me laughing so much.

I am Jehudiel, and I wish to pass my message to you all.

You who have caught the eyes of and ears of the Divine and us angels, and you who are blessed in their attention: Listen up!

You are the most bountiful and beautiful in your world, and yet you cannot see it within yourselves. You compliment others on their beauty and encourage it in others, which is indeed worth the joy in our lives. But we have noticed you don't give yourselves the same treatment. You are missing out a major factor in your lives.

You must also compliment yourselves. Appreciate your own beauty and light. You are more than just worth it. You need it, and it is also inspiring to better feelings. Look after yourselves and keep telling your spirit within you how beautiful it is, because it *is* beautiful. More than you can dream of. Your spirit has stood by you through thick and through thin. It is, in fact, an essential part of yourself. So love it, laugh with it, and above all embrace it. It is your inner self, your real personality. It is you! I'm not talking about the obsessive self-love that belongs to the vain; theirs is over the top. I'm talking about the self-love that accepts what you are, warts and all.

You already have a love of others around you, so you may as well give yourself some of yours. It is completing and necessary. Like the full circle, what you love about yourself will in turn make you more beautiful in our eyes. That, in turn, lets us love you back. So many of you have forgotten about this, and yet it is so vital. Don't let others put you down and take away your appreciation of yourself. It's none of their business. Let them look after themselves.

Gabriel and the others have been telling you this for a long time, and yet some still haven't quite got it. So I decided to butt in, as you would say. This is because I can speak plainer—a no-holds-barred wrestler of words. That is because words are one of my areas. Please listen and then look in that mirror. You know which one: that full length one. Say loudly to yourself and your inner spirit, "I love you inside and out! I am perfect in the Divine's eyes, I am perfect in the eyes of the angels, and I am perfect for myself."

Y'know what? It is because you really are perfect.

Now, get in front of that mirror!

I leave you with my message and my now laughing messenger. I am happy to make you all laugh. Yes, I'm laughing too.

Be light and love.

Jehudiel

During this message, I saw Jehudiel. Jehudiel shows as having long wavy brown hair, hazel eyes, and a cheeky grin. He is tall, wearing a white and silver robe. What I haven't written in the message was the nudges, cheeky comments, and exuberance that Jehudiel was giving me. There is a limit to what I put down here, and Jehudiel can be blunt to the point of tactless. He's just said laughingly, "I don't get out much!"

***

May 10, 2014

A message just came in from Michael.

> I see things, a lot of things, and some of which you would never see in your lifetime. Yet you do see a lot with your own eyes and ignore it. Stop right there! Open all your eyes, physical and spiritual, and see the world around you.
>
> Are not the clouds in the sky beautiful? Yes! Are the flowers and the trees equally beautiful? Yes!
>
> The beasts and insects that can fly, swim, and walk upon your world? They are beautiful too.
>
> And you? Are you beautiful?
>
> Yes!
>
> You are part of this world you walk upon, and therefore you are part of Gaia. You are beautiful in our eyes and Gaia's.
>
> Cherish the plants for their own ability and skills. They too can heal you.
> Love the animals, birds, and insects. They can help you.
> Look after your skies. They will sustain you.
> Above all, look after yourselves, for you will help yourself to grow to us.

Let this be so, my beautiful ones. Let this be so.

For nature is a strong force and is another name for the Divine. The Divine governs all of these, and even the lowliest creature was given to your world by the Divine. They all have their part to play, including you. Your part is to look after your world, to love and care for it. It is your home, and at this moment it will remain your only home while you are physical. Never sully your doorstep because it will damage your love. Look after your world, and it will look after you.

Be at peace with yourself, and you will find peace in your home. Let it happen. "Let what happen?" I hear you say. The answer is love.

Let it happen.

Amazing things have come about through love. That's why it is so much in demand. It beautifies, brings joy, peace, and completeness. Now, isn't that something to aim for? Don't hold back; let it flow like the veritable river. You will find things changing inside and out once you fully release yourself to love. You will find yourself growing spiritually, and others will be drawn to you and give love you back. This will help you all grow together.

Let it happen, beautiful ones.

Then all is well. Up where I am, we are treasuring your joyful experiences yet are willing to help when you call for us when you come across those difficult times. It has been said before and will be said again. If you have need of our help, ask us. Show us what you want in your mind and be detailed about it. Ask with love in your hands and heart. We will help, equal in love.

Let it happen.

I shall leave you now with my words. I am Michael. I am your helper in times of need, your friend in times of peace, and a brother in times of love.

Michael

***

May 13, 2014

A particularly long message from my teacher, Gabriel.

> You are not alone, my dear ones. You are not alone; you are never alone. No matter how far you have fallen in dark times, you will always have us watching over you. We will stand by you when all seems lost. We will catch you when you fall. You see, you needn't feel left out or secluded. We are here.
>
> Be assured of that. This is one of our blessings to you, the blessing of our love for you. That is why we are beside you no matter what happens to you. We are constant, like the air you breathe, like the river that flows. We are here for you and will forever remain by your side. This we do promise, my beloved ones.
>
> Let us give our love to you in its many forms. Some receive it as gifts of feathers from us. Others receive coins. But no matter how it is received, it is from us, and it is done to show we care, and we are beside you. Let us love you; accept our love. Accept our many assorted gifts.
>
> Some have already sensed our presence. A sensation of a hand stroking your cheek, a hand on your shoulder, or even a cool refreshing breeze around the face and hands is part of our signs. Ah, isn't it so beautiful?

All you need in this world is within you all, and we can help you reach that inner peace and joy. We can take away your darker moments and replace them with our love.

If your pain is that of loss, Azrael can share his compassion and love for you. Azrael's sweet, gentle love will enfold you in comfort.

Michael can chase away those negative energies who try to prey on you. Ask him to do this, and he will come with his sword and love.

Stresses in your job can be eased with the help of Jehudiel.

If you have any problems with sick pets or wild animals, Ariel can be of assistance there. Ariel loves those who love animals and will help you the best.

Metatron's clear mind can help you with memory, or to focus and open your inner light to the Divine. If you feel blocked spiritually, let Metatron help you.

Illness or other such health problems, Raphael has the best skill, even though Michael can nearly match him there. But you can call on either one, and they will heal with love and compassion. They are brothers indeed.

Gabriel can help with the arts and literature. Writer's block is not a problem.

If you find yourself unable to express yourself in words or pictures, let me help. I can also help with matters involving children, infants, and fertility.

Haniel will help women come into their spiritual essence and prime. Haniel helps women grow into their gifts of psychic and medium gifts. Just ask.

Zadkiel can help those who have problems with studying for exams. Just ask Zadkiel to help with memory problems.

Raziel will help those who are learning the higher levels of their spiritual gifts. Raziel is the teacher who will lead those who need to advance.

Chamuel will help you find your soul mate or a friend when you feel alone. Just ask, and all will be arranged.

Raguel will help those who have contention and hostility and who are argumentative. Raguel is the peacemaker and a mediator.

Jophiel is the joy bringer. Let Jophiel bring you to the light of happiness when you are sad, for music and laughter are strong gifts.

Sandalphon can help when you need music in your life and love. Sweet Sandalphon's love is like the rippling of harp strings. So soothing, gentle, and yet vibrant. He shall lighten your burdens when the heart is heavy.

Ezekiel shall bring you light when all you can see is darkness. Ezekiel is the fire when there is coldness. Follow his light, and you will find yourself out of your darkness.

That is enough, though I could go on. This is a list of those whom you can call when all is dark. Learn it well, beloved ones. Each of these angels await your love and attention.

I shall leave you now, dear ones.

Gabriel

***

May 14, 2014

It's been one of those days. I slept heavily through the night, and all day today I have had a feeling of hands pressing on my head hard, with a headache building up. It's still going on strong twenty-four hours later, and I'm feeling slightly out of it. I did a quick meditation in the hopes of grounding myself, just in case I needed it. This is what happened next.

I saw an angel standing in front of me, hands gently clasped in front and watching. The angel was dressed in robes of black and red. The face was very dark-skinned—native African, in fact. The hair was in long black dreadlocks. The face was beautiful and had a very wide, lovely smile, and the energy of this angel was of peace and gentleness.

We talked for a short while about my life path. The angel mentioned that I needn't worry because I was to leave one path and move onto another. There were a few other things spoken about, but I can't remember for the life of me. In the end, the angel asked if there were any questions I needed to ask. I asked if I was permitted to know its name. The angel replied, "Ezekiel."

I thanked the angel with love, and just before I left, I asked if he would like to give a message to everyone here through me sometime. The reply: "That is good!" and the beaming smile widened. I expect we will hear more from Ezekiel soon.

***

May 15, 2014

A message from an old friend, Zadkiel.

> Are you ready? Are you ready for the time of your spiritual life? Hold on, my friends; it's going to happen.
>
> You are on a roller coaster called life, and it goes up and down at high speed. The only difference is you can stop at any time. You can then walk away without any harm coming to you. This is what happens when you are changing from one life path to another. Take one step in a different direction than the one you were originally heading. That is your choice and free will at work there.
>
> Some think that all their problems are other people's fault. Your watch has stopped; blame the manufacturer. You spill your drink; blame the drink maker. Everyone else's fault but their own. That is negative, and such a mindset will pull you down. Let go of such, and you find that life for you will take a turn for the better. And that funfair called life will change into a free concert. Your body has its own music and beat, so dance to it. Your life, your choice; you deal with it.
>
> Please take responsibility for your own actions. In doing so, you will grow further and wiser. It is one of the first steps towards spiritual growth.

And when everything starts to come together in you, watch out, world—a new star has developed within you. Let it grow, and you will grow with it. You will find that your world will also grow with your own inner star. Strangers will become drawn to you as you are to them; you are glowing with the most important thing in this universe: love!

This includes the other stars around you. They too will be drawn to you because they will see you as a kindred spirit. The more stars that come into being and grow, the more your world will ascend. It is a fact of the Divine that the more you grow, the nearer you are to the Divine.

Let it be so and more. Yes, more! In the future, your world will become part of the light and will grow into the next stage: Creation. Oh, so many will grow, merge with the Divine, and grow again. It's a never-ending circle, and what a journey it will be. You have a future that is beyond your current understanding, but it will become clear to you in time.

Show me your inner light and let me add my light to yours. This is one thing I can do for you all, and I do it with love. Grow, my star children, and let yourself be seen for what you really are: beautiful!

Be blessed and be with the light.

Zadkiel

***

May 18, 2014

A message from a new teacher of mine: Metatron. (Yes, I have spiritually gone up a new level, and Metatron has taken over.)

Welcome to you all. Welcome to the great adventure that you call life. It is never the same for everyone. Every single individual will have his or her own needs met and catered to. You will be listened to by the most understanding of all: us.

Your life will be one great story amongst many tales. You can create your own beginning, plot, and ending. You are the book of which you write your story. That is the way of every mortal. When you have finished the last chapter in your life story, you leave and come to us for a rest. In time, you go back and start another sequel to your story with a lot more different range of characters. Take your current life. It is just a sequel to the one you had before. You write the book; you write your story. You are the story. That is a rather simplified way to describe the Akashic records.

As you write your book, your story is also being written in these records. You are the story, you are the book, and you are part of the Akashic records. That is the truth. That's why I ask you all to be careful of what you write in your story. Be aware that your actions to others are also being written down there. If you help others and fill their lives with love, it will be written down there. All of us can access this record. Some of your people can access the records too, but only their own, not others—yet.

Live your life with all the love and joy you can give to your selves and others. Be caring with those who are ill or need your sympathy. Show your love to your planet and those that live on it. These also will be written down in your story. This is your life. Live it like it is the most important and beautiful thing you can do physically. Live it all with the love and joy alive in you.

This pleases us. As you let all this energy of the light come into you, you are glowing with the pure love and happiness that is released within you. Do you know what you look like to us when you are glowing like that? You look like stars. You are miniature suns. Very beautiful indeed. That is the way to go, and when this light energy interacts with you on a cellular level, you will find your story will begin to change in another direction. That direction is towards the Divine.

This is the ultimate in your story. Please let yourself live and do it with love. We will share your joy and happiness with you. Such is your story; such as your record. You will become part of the great book of Divine love.

That is something we all look forward to.

I shall leave you now with my words to ponder on. Till the next time.

Love and light,

Metatron

***

May 19, 2014

I've been holding back on my artwork while I've been learning new shading techniques. My teacher Metatron asked me to do a sketch using the measuring techniques in a book. The result was naff. Then Metatron told me to draw in my usual freehand style with some of the shading ideas I've learned. I did this. I was already receiving an image of whom I was to draw. I asked if I was to know the name after the drawing, and I was informed yes.

At the end of the drawing, I asked who the model was. The reply was, "Me."

So here is the picture of my teacher who posed for me: Metatron.

***

May 20, 2014

A rare message from Archangel Haniel.

> Beautiful people, beautiful love. Sounds rather over the top to some, but to us it is perfect. You are those names: beautiful. Many things come under the name of beauty. The plants, the insects, the creatures that walk and swim in this world. Yes, that means you all. Even the rocks and the lakes are beautiful. In short, Gaia is your world and is you. And isn't she beautiful?
>
> Look around you. See Gaia's gifts to you all. A simple flower, and even a little bumblebee. These are all part of your world and one of the world's gifts. Treasure them. They're more valuable than all the gold and the diamonds. Treasure them. Believe in that which is within you also. Your spirit within is part of your world. It is your main part, and it is in touch with you. Your spirit is here to learn of you, including your world. This is all part of the path to the Divine.
>
> Treasure them.
>
> Golden years are not those memories that have long gone. They are instead now and in the future. You miss the past at times, but you may as well give up on that because the past is past and cannot and must not be brought back. Go forward and make your

future years yours to live, love, and believe in. Make them your golden years. Step forward, and you will grow. Live in the past all the time, and you will be left behind in the past. This is because you wished it to be, and so it will be. There is no harm in going forward, you know. No harm at all.

What is stopping you mostly is the fear of the unknown. But think about it: what do you have to fear? Some fear of being alone, which is ridiculous because we are always around watching, caring, and loving you. Some fear ridicule, that too is not true. We won't be mocking you; we will be helping you, coaxing, and supporting. Your fears are false, and we are always there for you. Throw away your fears and come forward. Your fears are just your ego telling you what it expects and what it has been told by other egos.

Surrender that ego to the past; let your subconscious come out. It will never lead you astray, it does not feel fear, and it doesn't need memories of a bad past. It is there for you now to help you look forward into the future. It seeks to preserve you and bring you into the light. Your spirit is your subconscious—your higher self, in fact. You are in its best interest.

Now, open yourselves to your glorious world and the golden future that awaits you. That future is for you alone. Be blessed in that you have our love and the Divine's love. We are here to help you on your path and will make sure that you will reach your destiny.

Your world has much to offer; accept it.
The Divine gave you so many gifts; accept them.

We love you unconditionally; accept it.
In return, we accept you.

Be within the Divine light of love.

Till the next time,

Haniel

***

May 23, 2014

A message from an angel who often speaks to us: Michael.

Dearest ones. I come to you to pass my message of love, compassion, and joy to all. Yes, that message is for all. It's love and understanding, give and take, close or far. This is a message to all of you.

You who are blessed in many ways should understand how wonderful you are, but you are unable to see yourselves. You are the very stars in your world, yet you are blind to your own light. That is a shame! For if you could see yourselves as we see you, you would be struck by wonder at your own beauty. Yet you seem not to see this light. You close your eyes to many things in your sphere of existence. You tie yourselves to your own physical world.

Well, stop! You can do so much more than what is in front of you. Open your eyes and look towards us, take us into your hearts. Then we will show you how magnificent your world is, and you will be able to see yourselves for what you are: part of the Divine. We too are part of the Divine, and so we are siblings. You don't have to be formal with us or standoffish. We are family, and we are of the family of the Divine. Like all elder siblings, we will help you when you struggle, pick you up when you fall, and hold you back when you step into the face of danger. We are a family. We are part of you.

It's rather a thought-provoking idea. Some of you never thought of us angels in that way. But when you do, it makes some sense, doesn't it? We understand more than you think, and we will make sure your spirit stays safe just by believing in us. We even look after those who don't believe in us. It is a job of love and one we will do.

"Why?" some ask. I'll tell you in one four-lettered word: love. That's why.

It's all one and only in the Divine's eyes. You are love, we are love, and the Divine is love. We are all creations of love, in all its aspects. Sounds rather good, doesn't it? I like it. Surrender yourself to this love. Stand outside with your feet in the grass and your hands to the air and say, "I'll accept Divine love, and I accept the Divine into my life. In return, I shall give the Divine my love and love the Divine for accepting me."

The Divine hears all and sees all. You will be noticed. We are the agents of the Divine, and we will send the Divine's message of love to you. No need to fear that, for sending such a message into oneself is painless. In fact, it can be rather pleasant and warm. Let us do this, and we will watch over you. This is meant to be, and it will be. For it is written in the stars and by the very hands of the Divine. It is so. Be one with the Divine, and the Divine is within you. Be blessed in this for it is meant to be.

Join us in loving the Divine. We will share this duty with you and share it well. It is such a wonderful experience and such a blessing to us all.

Be blessed, my siblings. I wish you well in life and in love.

Michael

***

May 25, 2014

A message I received, but I had difficulty in catching the name of the messenger. I managed in the end. Now, this is the first time I've spoken to Cassiel, who let me know this morning that there was a message to me to give.

> Thank you! Thank you for coming to read this, my message to all.
>
> Do not let negativity enter your hearts, for it will bring nothing but sadness into your lives. Let the positivity of joy and laughter enter instead; you will find your world will become a much better place.
>
> Before your birth, you were given a choice. Do you wish to laugh or cry in this current life? Either way, you will learn the same lesson. But the way you chose how to live it is yours alone. It's not too late to change your mind. You can choose to laugh any time you want. Let us help you with that. Let us help. Laughter is precious and much loved by us, for it brightens your spiritual self and your lives. Even the Divine treasures laughter. It is precious; it is more than gold. It is light!
>
> Is it too late for you to remove the negativity in your lives? No!
> Is it too late to move away from those who would pull you down in sadness? No!

Is it too late to let go what is no longer wanted or needed? No!

That's right! It's never too late, and the moment you decide it becomes the right moment. The doors to the paths of light are never locked against you. They are closed, but they are never locked. All you need to do is open that door yourself. It's not hard.

Loved ones, I hear your words and feel what you feel. Never let such pain and sorrow own you, for they should never do that. Let love own you. That is the real owner of your heart. Yes, owner! And love is Divine, and the Divine is love. Let it come into your life, sweet ones. Embrace all the wonders and beauty of the world, and the greatest of all, the Divine. You can never go wrong in your life if you let the Divine and us into your lives. We can supply all the joy, happiness, and beauty in your life. The Divine can create all this for you alone.

Each one of you is different, and each person receives that love differently, but the result is the same. Oh, it is so beautiful to watch others completely and totally embrace the Divine into their hearts. Your aura is like a rainbow when that happens, and it shines so much brighter.

I have to say you have all done wonderfully and come so far in this lifetime. There's more to come in future lifetimes, but don't let that worry you. Things will get interesting, but we will be here to guide you along your path.

Daughters, love the one who has earned it. That love will remain pure. Your offspring is another step of humanity to our presence. Sons, treasure your wives, for they alone are the greatest future of your world. Treasure each other and nurture your love, joy, and happiness. It is best shared with someone close.

I bless you all, my beautiful ones. Enjoy your wonderful love and joy. It is all yours to share, and it is unlimited by time and space. It is ours. Be free in spreading your love, my children. Be free. You are the future and the past, the present and the now. Cherish your own children; they're there for you.

I shall leave you now and let you be free,

Bless you, children of the light.

Cassiel

***

May 27, 2014

A message from Ezekiel, who did say he would send me one soon.

> Blessed ones. You have grown so much, yet you have left so much behind. You have left behind your youthful innocence.
>
> Children are innocents and are to be treasured. They have open minds and a very active imaginations that need to be encouraged. Don't force them to give up their dreams or lose their love of life. Help them to live it more by helping them do things they love. If children show the ability to be an artist, let them learn it. They will love their art, and we will feel their joy as they show their imagination on a piece of paper.
>
> Let children grow up with that joyfulness unabated. Let them have their imagination. After all, a lot of things in your world would not have been invented if it wasn't for imagination—such things like aeroplanes, bicycles, hot air balloons, music, and dancing. All are items of joy and imagination.
>
> See, this is what I meant by you keeping your own youthfulness instead of losing that childlike love of beautiful things. If you are as children before the Divine, you will be doubly blessed, for that is the perfection we seek within your mind and spirit. And after all, children are beautiful to us both. You are as

children to us in that you have much to learn, and we will teach you to learn the beauty of your world and ours. That is what we want for you. Learn, sweet ones, learn.

Growing that childlike wonder into your own body will bring you so much beauty in your world. We will cherish you indeed. Let go of your worries and stresses; they will stop you from reaching this goal. Let it all go, and instead let yourself go within the embrace of nature.

You are our children; you are our past and our future. You are your own beloved receptacles of love. Is it any wonder why we love you all so? Yes, we do love you that much. We only want you to live your life to the fullest, and with all the joy you can muster. Your happiness is what makes us all happy with you.

Beloved ones, be with us in love and spirit, and we will be with you by your side, watching over you in spirit. We will protect you from hidden attacks and warn you if you go wrong.

Let this be so, my beloved ones.

Ezekiel

***

May 28, 2014

Here is a brief channelling for everyone.

> Now is the time to let go of all your problems and your worries. Let the universe have them for in the eyes of the Divine; your problems are small and can be overcome. Ask, and you will feel your answer. Your answer will lie within you, and secretly you already know what it is.
>
> That is the Divine answering you because the Divine is also within you.
>
> Be well.
>
> Gabriel

***

May 29, 2014

A message from Sandalphon to you all.

We speak again, my friends. We meet again too. How was your day? Think on this and then read on.

Was your day a good day with laughter, fun, light, love, or even business that is finally finished? If so, well done. You have lightened your soul with all these good things. You have healed it a bit. You have learned to raise your spiritual level. Well done indeed!

Was your day a boring day in that nothing happened, but instead you decided to chill out and relax from the rat race? That is good also. You are relaxing and recharging your energy for the next day. We all need to have days like that on occasion. You have learned to relax, let go, and let God. It all helps in the healing process.

Was your day a bad day? Things went wrong in some way—perhaps a fight or an accident? In a way, that too was a day that was necessary. It is then a day of learning. Such incidents happen so that you may learn from them. Learn them well and heed them, and they won't happen again.

See? Every day you are learning something new or old.

If you are learning new stuff, then you have taken a step forward in life. This is to be commended. Keep on learning.

If you are repeating bad choices and miserably, you obviously haven't learned anything. Well, you never will unless you open your eyes and look at what is around you. You don't have to make those bad issues happen. You can both learn from them and walk away.

Never hold onto negative energies or situations. Sever all attachments from this harmful incident, learn from the experience, and leave. Let it go. And if you have learned the correct lesson and heeded it, things will get better for you. Such incidents only repeat if you don't learn from it.

Beloved ones, I tell you this so that you may wake up your mind and open your eyes. You are all learning a vast and valuable lesson. Learn well and take it to heart. Memorize the problem and what was the cause; then learn not to make a mistake again. You do learn from mistakes made in the past and present. Learn it all.

All will be revealed in time as to why you are learning all this. You won't be at a loss. Grow, learn, absorb, and go forward. As you learn more, the greater will be your strength and inner spirit. Let go and let God.

I thank you for your patience and love,

Be blessed, my loved ones.

Sandalphon

***

June 1, 2014

A message from an archangel that I have spoken to before, but a long time ago.

> Beloved sweet ones. This is a message to all. It is a message of peace, awareness, and love. You are the recipients of it all. I shall pass this message on.
>
> You who are beloved in the eyes of the Divine are blessed.
>
> You were all given gifts of such wonders as love, joy, laughter, and awareness. You are all blessed in that. Please enjoy those gifts that were given to you. They are now yours to use and share. Don't hide them away, don't ignore them. They can't be hidden because they are embedded deep within your heart and are forever finding ways to manifest. You may as well let these gifts have full reign over you. You won't regret it one little bit when you feel filled with such wonder and happiness.
>
> These are the gifts that are for you all. Love them, love each other, and love yourselves. They will all bring you much joy.
>
> Is not the child in front of you a product of love? Look in the mirror, and you will see the child within you. You are the child of love. You are the child of

our blessings. And what a beautiful child you are then and now. Yes, you!

My child of dreams, you have come to be because there is a task to perform. And when you have performed it, you will find yourself closer to us in enlightenment. You will find you can spread your spiritual wings over a lot of people, who will in turn help you spread your love further.

One simple word describes this process: love.

We wish you to spread this as much as possible, in the hopes that more and more will become in tune with our presence. In this, miracles will occur. You are one such miracle. Well done! Share your miraculous self with love and understanding. Be patient with those who do not understand, because in turn they will learn and will need to turn to you for support.

Be trustworthy so that others may place their trust in you and will give you their support in turn.

Be joyous so that others may spread the joyful note of the singing in your heart.

Be blessed, o that others may share their blessings and love with you.

I could go on so much regarding this miracle that is you, for you are all that and more. What I can say! There are many stories, truths, hope, and happiness that is within you and the child you are inside your soul.

Go forward, my child of dreams; go forward and upwards. Your dreams are your future reality. Dream on and grow. You will be that dream. You are someone else's dream.

You are blessed by the Divine and us.

Raguel

***

June 2, 2014

I felt an urge to do another message, and so I tuned in. This time I got Uriel. He had a message for us all, as well as a little private one for me.

Greetings, all.

I am here today to let you all know of something wonderful that is coming soon. It's so wonderful that you will find yourself growing with it.

I let you discover the power of the Divine coursing through you. This power is cleansing, purifying, and above all enlightening. Let no one interfere with this process because it is a delicate process that will take some of your free time. Let it be known that you have received this gift and that you have been given the ability to use it.

Open, my children. Let the world of the Divine enter your hearts. Believe in yourself as you are perfect as you are. Believe in others for they can be your greatest allies in times of worry. Believe in the Divine, for the Divine can use this gift to help you. Love is one aspect of this gift. The other aspect is you. You are part of this gift also. Let love, let you, let go, and let God. That phrase says it all. Let us in and let us help.

Beloved ones, let your sword be that of the light and powered by your lives and love. Let your defence be that of enlightenment, so that you may resist all negative energies that will sap at you. Let it be so, my beloved ones. Let it be so. I am Uriel, and I say this is so.

I shall have my own sword of light to help remove negative thoughts towards you. Michael has his sword to remove any negative energies that have attached themselves to you. That is the way it is and will be. We are both standing guard over you and your family. We do this in the name of love. Will you deny us from protecting you? I hope not.

The sweetest honey in the world cannot compare to the sweetness of the Divine presence. For the Divine rules us all, you and me. We will ensure that no one can remove you from the Divine love. It is, after all, your right to feel it and belong to it. We too can feel it; it is wonderful. Please step up and forward, let the light of the Divine shine upon you, and let it take over your lives. You will learn and grow in this light. It will sustain you and defend you from all those who will harm you.

Beloved ones, never let yourself go, for in doing so, you are cultivating your negative side. Look after yourself and let none try to take your own personal power away from you. If people do, remove them from your life, for they are no longer serving their purpose for you, and it is time for you to move on. Let it be so. I am Uriel, and I say it will be so.

***

June 6, 2014

A message from an archangel that I never expected. I asked if any wanted to pass a message, and I felt a presence indicate he wanted to. His energy felt different, and I got the sensation of someone standing behind me and putting his hands on my shoulders. That soon became a feeling of a hand stroking my head. Part of the message is private and for me alone; I have not written it here.

Here is a message from Nathaniel.

> Blessed be. This is indeed an experience I have done and felt many a time. Passing messages through you is a wonderful thing. I am glad you let me have permission. I love you.
>
> Now for my message, sweet one.
>
> I am pleased to speak to you all. I bring my love to you in all hope that it will be reciprocated. Yes, I do love you all. You see, you do not need to fear me or what I do. I am a part of love, just like you. We are all part of the One Source. The One Source is who you call the Divine. The One Source is also called the Creator and Creation.
>
> There are many names for such a magnificent, powerful entity. But the one we know and welcome the most is love.

Yes, you are beginning to see. I have asked to pass on my message so that you all may know a little bit about my world and my essence. Therefore it is hard to see us; we are made of energy that is not part of your dimension, but of Creation. This is something you need to know, for you too will in time become part of the Divine, part of Creation. Just like me. Let me assure you that you will find such exhilaration and joy when that happens. The sights and sounds are much more different to us than they are to you. It's an experience you really need to look forward to.

I cannot describe it too well because there are no words in your many languages that can accurately mention such things. The nearest I can find is nirvana. Some call it heaven. It is rather heavenly in many ways.

Oh, if only you knew how I feel right now. Such love, joy, and happiness—and it's all there, and I can feel it. It is also waiting for you, and I would love to have you experience such a wondrous thing. I await that moment with such love and anticipation, for I would love to see your faces when you feel these sensations. It is well worth seeking. Seek out these experiences. They will be waiting for you when you ascend.

Bless you all. I am Nathaniel, and I await your pleasure in my world. Let it be so, and so much more.

Beloved ones, you have much more of your paths to go to, but you have journeyed far on your current one. Keep going, keep loving, and keep your hopes high. We will help you and await your arrival. Be blessed; I know of this, and I too will wait.

Nathaniel

***

June 9, 2014

Here is a message from Metatron for everyone. Just come in hot from the angel.

> I welcome you all back to my presence. Your words have been heard by my colleagues and me. You have asked for help, and you have been heard. You have called for us, and that we do appreciate. I thank you.
>
> You have a world so beautiful that glows like a jewel in the stars. That is a true beauty. Your spiritual selves are strong and shine rainbows. You are all beautiful inside, so ignore what others say to lower you. In doing so, they are inadvertently lowering themselves. Glow, my children.
>
> You are indeed lucky. You are gifted. You are beloved. We have kept our trust and our promise; we will nurture you. This is a time of great strides towards advancement. We will keep on watching, listening, and loving you. As always, we are at your side. We are always walking with you.
>
> Beloved ones, you are learning new things every day—things that will help you grow, help you develop and above all, help you to believe. We only ask that you believe in yourselves, and we will believe in you. Nothing is set in stone, as you know. If you want to change your life, it is never too late in our eyes and the Divine's. Call us, and we can make this an easy journey for you—easier than you can imagine.

Let love be your guide and let us be your guardians. You are children to us, for that is what you are in comparison to the other levels of ascension. You are at the child stage. This is the best stage of all to learn the basic rules of ascension, for it is the easiest then. Let this be so and let you believe in yourself, your family and your closest friends. You are our children. You are our beloved ones. You are the future of the universe.

This advancement in the universe has one destination. The ultimate destination: you will be the Divine. The children of our children will also be our children. You who are brighter than the stars will know this, for those are the ones more advanced in ascension. Those who do not glow as bright, your turn will come. I can truly guarantee this. It is your destiny and truth. You are also our little brothers and sisters. Let not this be the end of our relationship, for even high in advancement, we need each other. This need is called love. And we continue to help you because of that.

Grow well, my beloved ones. You have a great and wondrous future ahead of you. So please don't ruin it by walking into the darkness, for that is truly the path of extinction. Choose wisely, my beloved ones. You have the choice of the universe in your hands.

Be well.
Be true.
Believe.

Metatron

***

June 12, 2014

A message from an archangel that I love working with: Gabriel.

> Delightful, isn't it? The way the sky looks at night when the moon is glowing. The light of peace and serenity from it pools around you. If you go farther into the universe, the stars will be the guiding lights there. So many and yet so magnificent in their appearance. The universe is infinite, and so is the Divine.
>
> And did you know that you are too?
>
> Some of you have not realised this, but you too have infinite abilities. We all start small and grow from there. Just like the universe. By learning about your life, your world, and what is beyond the third dimension, you are growing bigger. In time you will grow to the point where you can only move up the ladder of destiny and grow there. This is how humans will evolve. The next dimension is the next stage of humanity's growth. For it is a stage nearer to the Divine. The Divine is all dimensions, all states, and the universe.
>
> Well, do you see what I am aiming at? I am trying to help you all grow into your future destiny. It is a world of beauty and amazing effects. A world where the boundaries of your life have been reduced. You

can explore safely and be welcomed into the realm of ascension.

This growth will help you in reaching us easier. That is much admired. We want this to happen, and we will help you in making this path smoother for you.

Let it be so.

Just open your hearts, your minds, and your love to us. We will take care of the petty things and leave the wondrous part of your adventure to you. This is all you need to do, as it is the best part and you will enjoy it the most if you do it yourself. We won't let you struggle because the hard part will be taken care of by us, and we will help in teaching you the easiest method that will make it work for you. You just sit back, meditate, and learn. That's all your part involves.

Simple as that. No more and no less.

Now, is it time for you to give us a call? To ask us to take away a burden that lies heavy on your heart? That is the first step in your growth, and to be honest, it's an important one. This step tells us that you are now growing into your spiritual self and opening up. Let your guardian angels be your guide and protector, for they will watch over you constantly. They know when you have problems and can ease them for you. They can call upon us if there is a big problem that is beyond them. You see, you are not alone in this path of life. You will never be alone. There is always someone watching over you, caring and loving. We all have your best interests at heart and will never abandon you.

If you want to talk to us, then speak from your heart. We will give your answer via your heart. That is what our voice is. If you even ask the Divine itself, The Divine will hear you. Your answer from the Divine will also come to you from your heart, as the Divine is within you all. The Divine is within us all, and we are all aspects of the Divine. Angel or human, we are all from the Divine. We call you our children.

Let it be so.

Blessed ones, it is time for me to let go of my messenger.

You have my blessing and my love, sweet ones.

Gabriel

Note: They call us their children because we are the children of the Divine, but we are in the care of our teachers: The Angels. They are also our siblings, but when they are teaching us, they call us their children, as in pupils.

***

June 15, 2014

Another message, but this time by an angel I've never heard of. I can't find any record anywhere of this one. There is a humorous, private message for me from Michael at the end, but I'm keeping that private.

> This is strange, this is unusual. This is wonderful!
>
> I speak to you for the first time. I am Messera; I am of the higher realm. I speak to you of the wonders that are to come to your world. The wonders of light and life. You will be amazed at what will happen very soon.
>
> Some of you will grow to the next level. Others will shift into dimensions. But more will expand and grow further in your own world.
>
> This growth will be expected and will show you that there are no limits to your own abilities. Your mind, vision, and insight will grow too.
>
> You are developing your sixth and seventh senses. That is your growth.
>
> The angels have called upon me to pass this message to you all, and I heartedly agree that it is now due. I am Messera, the higher lord of the third level. I welcome you to your amazing future, and I hope to see more of you.

Let it happen, my future companions and friends. Let us greet our new future together. Please open your inner eyes and mind; let nothing tie you down. Your spirit and visions can roam free in this universe of yours.

Make this universe your home for your spirit; it is there for you to move into and around. Feel free and let your mind expand into new paths and thought. We welcome you all, wondrous ones.

Yes, I said *we*. I am Messera, an angel of life. I am the protector of trust and the giver of gifts. I am also Messera, who loves you all freely.

I hold out my hands, and in them are the gifts of the light, peace, and the future. These gifts are in the form of seeds that grow into plants, which live in the light, flourish in Peace, and grow more fruits to feed the mind of the future. This is my—no, *our* gift to you all.

Michael, my brother, take over now because I must now prepare the way.

Bless you all.

Messera

***

I am Michael. You have heard the words of Messera. Heed them, for they are words that will open new paths for you. Messera rarely speaks to those in your world because he is always busy in his part of the light. He holds the garden in his domain and protects it from the darkness. He looks after the garden in the hopes you will rejoin him again. Will you join him? You have journeyed far on your path; I think you will.

I welcome you and bless you. Let the light shine in, and let it plant the seeds of your future grow within you. I await your pleasure in this.

Bless,

Michael

***

June 17, 2014

Woo-hoo! I was contemplating on the universe and the spiritual origins when I found my mind shifting, and I saw myself as part of the universe. I suddenly began saying, "I am part of the universe, and the universe is part of me. I can do anything I want in this universe, and I have that ability. I can grow outwards and upwards. The universe and I are one." My mind expanded into the vastness of the universe.

I saw a galaxy begin to form in front of my third eye, and an angel was standing amongst them. Both the galaxy and the angel were one. A flow of intense energy then shot through me at this time, and my mind felt like it was floating and trying to reach beyond the skull.

Right now, I'm still on a kind of high.

I'm back. I just asked the angels if this was what they were waiting for, and I was told it was. Apparently, the energy peaked a bit. After this, I ended up crying not with sadness but with a feeling of being overwhelmed. It quickly passed, and I'm still feeling bursting at the seams with energy.

I've asked my guardian angel, and she said, "Growth." My other guardian angel said, "Your will." They informed me that my path and existence is the Divine's will and that I work with the Divine's will. And that is meant to be for me. My will and the Divine's are one, in that I bring the messages of the angels. We both want that. Gabriel has just told me that I've gone up a level—hence the energy surge.

Oh, boy. Normally I'm sleeping when that happens. I knew I was close but didn't realise how close I was.

My head now feels as if there was an energy field surrounding the crown. If it could be seen, I suspect that field would be shining around my head like a glowing aura field.

I've just asked an angel what it looked like and was shown. Yep! Seemingly it's stretching out thirteen to fourteen inches from my head. The auric field looks like a halo. Oh, boy! Still on a high—wee!

***

June 19, 2014

A wee update.

As you all know, I've gone up a level. I didn't know what new talent I'd have in doing so. Well, now I know. I can see the angels much more clearly—in fact as soon as I close my eyes, I see them as if they are as solid as you and me. They move about as we do in them. Their faces are hard to see because they put on so many forms. Their faces seem to shift and change and then settle on one, and that one I'll see. What doesn't change is their eyes. They talk with telepathy, which is also hyped up in me.

You see, it started earlier today when I decided to do some meditation. I never got there. As soon as I closed my eyes, I was surrounded by angels. All were facing towards me and watching. This was my first lesson: I had to face each one and name them. This was to help me match a name to face. During this, Michael turned up and walked towards me, smiling. Wow, he's tall! He bent over me and gave me a huge bear hug. He backed off and watched while I did my lesson.

One angel sitting beside me on my right reached over and put his hand on the top of my right hand. I could feel the touch. As I named him, I looked over to this angel and knew his name: Zadkiel. The other angels were around the room. Gabriel was at the back and leaning against a wall, watching. Chamuel came forward, a big grin on face and a pink glow around him. Raphael was sitting on my left side, and Haniel was beside him. Sandalphon was beside Zadkiel. Metatron was a bit behind. Azrael was a bit farther back.

There were a few archangels that weren't there.

When I finished, Haniel bent over me and said, "You're the one." The others appeared to be agreeing with Haniel. One by one, they all looked at me in the eye and said, "Love!"

I got another image of me walking down a passageway, through doors, and then down a hallway. I went through another set of doors and into a theatre. There was a glow in front of me, leading the way onto the stage, and I found myself facing the stage. The glow had grown larger and hovered over my head.

When I came back, they all asked if I would agree to be not only their voice but the voice of the One. I agreed, and that pleased them all. They all left except for Michael, who again walked up to me, gave me another hug, and gave me a kiss on the forehead.

Then I opened my eyes.

All this happened when I was in fact wide awake!

I quickly closed my eyes again and saw Michael leaning against a wall. I asked could I also see my guardian angels and my guides like this, and he said yes. I asked my guardian angels to show themselves. Darryl is a good-looking one who likes beards, has a calm nature, and has no BS with him. Fleur is very pretty and has a fun nature. I asked for my healing angel and guide and found Meriel in front of me, wavy, shoulder-length chestnut hair; a big, wide grin; and a mischievous glint in the eyes.

I was told that in time, I'd be able to see all of them with my eyes open.

Things are happening.

***

June 20, 2014

A message from my healing angel and guide Meriel.

> Well, this is to be said. Thank you for allowing me to enter your mind. And thank you for your offer and acceptance.
>
> Let us now speak of matters of the heart and mind.
>
> For all of you who read this, I know how hard life can be and how hard you yourself can make it for your own self. It doesn't have to be that way. All is an illusion, and you can unmake the unhappiness that you have made for yourself. You don't have to live a life that is negative; you can walk away and be in the light. A relationship that has gone sour is a sign that it is time to move on. A friendship that has dissolved means that both people have gone on their separate paths in life and no longer need each other for support. It is all part and parcel of learning in your lifetime. Learn so that you may know what to do and what is the meaning.
>
> Follow the light if you have to leave a bad situation. When you do that, your riches will grow. The richness of the soul is that of the purest white; it is a soul that embodies the Divine strongly. As I said, the hardness of your life is an illusion that you can remove from your eyes and walk into the reality of the light.

Have a fear of dying alone? Never! While we angels exist, you will never be alone. We are around you all the time, giving you love and support.

Have a fear of the outdoors? Ask us, and we can show you the way to love your world of beauty and wonder. We will keep you safe and strong.

Have a fear of enclosed spaces? You don't need to fear them because we will open your mind to a wider realm. Ask us to remove that fear. Yes, you simply need to ask us to remove any fear. Nothing is as bad as your imagination makes it out to be. Fear is part of the illusion that your imagination has made, and your imagination can remove it. That is why we can help you. We love your imagination, but when it has no control, then your fears appear.

Gain control of your imagination and your mind, hold it within your grasp, and only let it flow at a gentler level. The imagination is like the river. Too big, and it runs fast and out of control. Put up a dam, and it will hold back the fears. This is your opportunity to grab those fears and redirect them into something positive. Anger can be turned into determination. Fear can be turned into compassion. Depression can be turned into art and serenity. Then when you have done this, release the new feelings gently into the world and watch your world turn into the light.

It is all about balance, and you are the catalyst. Transform your world from that of darkness and come into the light just by transformation. You can do this; I know you can. And when you do, you will find that you can't stop. You will grow more and more into the light. It is all about your growth mentally, emotionally, and spiritually. They are connected, just like you relate to us.

We want you to succeed and grow into our love. And why? Well, for one we love you, and for another so does the Divine. You are perfect in our eyes, and we want you to be perfect in yours. Let us do that: help you.

Be blessed, for we will bless you with our love and compassion. The Divine wants you to be their torch of love. Again, be well, be blessed, and be yourself. Let no one take away your power. Take control of your own power and be a part of the Divine's light.

I thank you.

Meriel

***

June 23, 2014

A quick message from Archangel Chamuel.

> Some of you think you know it all, got it all, and lived it all. Guess what? It's only just started for most you. You've only just scratched the surface of your future, and it's going to be one long lesson for you all. Some parts will be hard; most will be easy. In the end, there is only one answer to all the lessons, and it all lies within you.
>
> You are the answer.
> Become the answer.
> Love is the answer.
>
> What is stopping you now?
>
> Chamuel

***

June 26, 2014

Yep, restless nights are starting again. I'm rousing up from sleep and sensing the angels around me again. They're downloading information into me. I roused up during the night, realised what was being taught to me, and said a silent "What the …?"

Raziel simply butted in with one word: "Learn!"

Do I really need to know how to expel an unwanted spirit from its victim's body—that is, exorcism? Hmm! I don't want to know, but the angels seem to think so. I'll probably forget as usual.

Meditation has the same treatment.

Earlier on, I was told about an angel called Chamodiel. Can't find any record of that name anywhere. I was told to be aware of him, but I roused up and lost the rest of the info. I asked what was going on, and again Raziel said, "Learn!"

I wish I knew what the heck was going on!

***

June 27, 2014

A message just came in hot from Archangel Michael.

> I greet you, my friends. I am Michael, and I wish to pass my message to you. Yes, all of you!
>
> As your world goes through space and time, taking all wonders of stardust and motes from other worlds that have passed by before you, think on this. They too were created by the Divine. They too had promises made on them, and all were created perfect. In time, they served their purpose in their mission and were made into dust again. Their mission? Ah, that is the surprise. Their mission was to create the merest speck of the first building blocks of perfection: you!
>
> You are made of this stardust, and as your race grew and developed, you took in more and more of this stardust. There is no shortage of the stuff of life. It is around you, in you, and floating freely in space too. The Divine created this stardust to build you—hence all this perfect material in you. No wonder you are perfect right now.
>
> I could go on and on about this topic, but I know I don't want to bore you. Heh!
>
> Ah, you wonderful, wonderful people. How I delight in your music and humour. How I want

this to be more common. You make me laugh with your jokes. You make me sing with your music. Your art is beautiful. I take great pleasure in this, so why do you restrict yourselves in this area? The arts are a gift from the Divine itself. It is a pure form of pleasure that even we actively partake in. You too must spend more time in this area, as it is very uplifting to the spirit and your vibrations increase. Also, take more time to laugh and enjoy life in all its many aspects, even if it is laughing at the antics of a small animal. They too are having fun in what they are doing. Even the deadliest of beasts on your world knows how to play. Play is good for you too because it is fun.

Play, laugh, sing, dance, and love! These are all good things and are the main source of your growth.

As you grow, we will help you.
As you sing, we will create your inner music.
As you dance, we will hold you upright.
As you laugh, we will create the fun.
As you love, we will energize you.
As you play, we will play with you.

So it must be, and you must realize that all is meant to be enjoyed in life. All are meant to be laughter and fun. You are all that and more, my beautiful ones. Play with your friends and laugh with them too. Enjoy life and all that is within it. It was made for you to take delight in, and we do appreciate your happiness. Why? Because of one thing: love!

And it is all for you.

Be well, my blessed friends.

Michael

***

June 30, 2014

I did some more experimenting with shading. I was told by Metatron to draw the impression I had received, and they didn't tell me the name of my model. It was only when the drawing was finished that I asked and got the name: Azrael.

Must say my sketching is improving greatly.

***

June 30, 2014

A message from Gabriel. Take note: Gabriel did not mince words in this one. archangels tell it like it is, as always:

> Beloved ones, let me call you that, for you are beloved to me.
>
> I come with a message for all and sundry. A message even the stars will notice. A message that says: It is time!
>
> It is time for you to open your hearts to your fellow man. It is time for you to embrace all within this world of yours, so that you may become part of the collective called the light.
>
> It is time for you to all to give your love to each other without any conditions. It is time for spiritual growth.
>
> As you are now, all is discord. Unity and peace cannot grow in such an environment. That discord is the way of darkness. So please stop all this hurt and pain that is inflicted on each other, and instead give each other your hand and heart in loving harmony.
>
> That is what I wish for. That is what I want and need. It is what we all want and desire. But you are stopping it from happening because of war, poverty, and despair.

The wars are of your own making, so you can stop it.

Poverty is also of your own making; again, you can stop it.

Despair and depression? Yes, you are making it too. Again, you can stop it.

You can stop all this by taking responsibility for your own actions and ceasing such negativity. Stop blaming others for your own faults. Deal with these faults. Learn from them. Understand them and then leave such faults behind, as you will no longer have a use for them. That is a single step towards growth.

Then once learned, step forward and accept the new paths of beginnings that will happen, beginnings that are beneficial to you. Those paths lead to harmony, spiritual growth, and of course the Divine.

Let your hearts open to each other so that you may discard the negative ways. Step off the path of self-destruction and move to the path of self-construction. Your world would be the better for it, and so will you. You will find that if you look after your world and your own self, the world will look after you in more ways than one. We are also part of your world, and so we too will be looking after you.

I hope I have given you all something to think about, for it is necessary for me to give you all a wake-up call. You must wake up and be strong, for you are the start of new beginnings, and you must encourage.

Life is not cheap at any cost. Life is priceless, and some cheapen it by their actions. This is not good and must be rectified. You must treasure each other; give love and take love with no conditions in it at all. You are all precious. Just be!

I know I had to tell you this, but you must admit things are not all well on your world.

I call my lightworkers to envision world peace and harmony, to manifest it. I call my lightwarriors to defend the lightworkers from all negative energies.

I call my messengers to deliver the words of the Divine and the angels, to encourage the light.

I call upon all of humanity to rise, grow, love, and become part of the Divine's light.

That is your destiny—don't forget that.

I give you all my love and blessing; I know you can make this work. After all, aren't you all versatile human beings?

I pass this message by Divine action and Divine love. You are the most important thing in this world, but remember that your world is the most important thing to you. Love the world, love each other, and love yourself unconditionally, just like we do. Go forth and spread your Divine light.

Be blessed, sweet ones.

Gabriel

***

July 1, 2014

Another musing of mine about how I came into this channelling lark.

All mediums can channel the angels. The angels will use those mediums to get their message across, but they don't use all those mediums all the time. Most of the mediums go on channelling spirits of those who have passed on. But there are some mediums who channel angels non-stop. For example, me. I am surrounded by them every hour of the day.

How can that be?

I was like most mediums and would channel passed ones. But Archangel Raphael chose me to pass a message through—twice! This time I felt an urge to say out loud, "I dedicate myself as a tool for whatever the angels wish me to be!" This was the trigger, and the angels took me up on that willingly. Since then, they have used me as their messenger.

Gabriel has taught me how to use my ability, and strengthens other psychic gifts, and likes to play harmless jokes on me.

Michael is frequently visiting me and is like a big brother to me: protective, humorous, and loving. He likes to sneak up and startle me.

Raziel has been teaching me more advanced spiritual knowledge during the night. Some people say there is something wizardly or witchy about me, even though I don't practice wiccan but respect it.

Jophiel has been making sure I don't sink into the black hole of depression, and he's doing a magnificent job at it. Jophiel's humour helps there.

Haniel mothers me and is not above telling me off if I do something stupid. Haniel looks after me and offers advice.

Raphael keeps prodding me to look after myself and has assigned a healing angel to teach me the art of healing. I can do chakra healing now. Thank you, Angel Meriel, for that.

Azrael has been a gentle and caring friend to me, always willing to chat. Now if only he'd quit the bad puns.

Jehudiel visits now and then to encourage me to work, and his effervescent energy is stimulating.

Chamuel likes to sit with me and chat. He has taught me to be accepting of all and to love unconditionally. He likes to say goodbye with a blast of his energy of pure love. That one nearly knocks me out of my seat, and he knows it. Cheeky!

Ariel is rarely around, but she knows that I care for the plants and animals, and she hears me when I need help in that area.

I could go on!

The trigger is to offer yourself to the angels—unconditionally! They will take you up on that offer, but don't be surprised if they use you in a capacity other than what you expected. They know what you are best at and will use that ability.

***

July 2, 2014

A rare message from the beautiful Haniel.

> This a message that I can give you. A message of understanding.
>
> You feel as if you are missing something. you are not.
>
> You feel as if you are sinking; you are not.
>
> You feel lost in your world; you are not.
>
> The reason why you are not any of these is that you aren't lost, but you are waiting. Yes, waiting for the right time and moment. The moment is called perfection. Anything outside that is doomed to fail, and so we want to make sure it doesn't—hence the "perfect" moment. Be patient and be strong in will, for the wait will try you out. This is necessary, for those who wait and endure will gain better from the wait. They shall have their reward. Those who can't wait and move away will lose out. Patience is a virtue, remember?
>
> So be patient, my loved ones. Things will happen, and they will happen at the right time, not before or after. There is much to learn while waiting—even waiting is a lesson in self-discovery. Some of you may find that while waiting, you already have your answer deep within you. That is because the answer has come to you at the right time. When that happens, understanding and release from your

vigil will occur. Your reward? The lesson in patience and understanding is the reward, and another step taken to your ultimate destination: the light. That is a reward well worth waiting for.

Now, do you understand what I mean by things coming at the right time? They will not be rushed or delayed. They are inevitable. You may as well raise your arms in acceptance and let them come.

There is much to be learnt on your path of self-discovery, so take it all one step at a time. You will learn all you need in your current lifetime, so there is no rush. Patience, remember? While waiting, why not enjoy your world, sing, and share your love? May as well make the wait well worth it. And again, it all helps towards your perfect moment. Dance for us and let us hear your voices raised in joy, not anger. Rest your hearts in an aura of peace. Let the laughter of children be your music of love. We all treasure such moments, and even when you were a child, we enjoyed your voices. Be a child for us again and let your love and happiness run free again. Enjoy the moment and enjoy the brightness of your inner light blossoming. A child is the most innocent thing in your world. Be that child so that we may take much pleasure in your company. Such innocence within you would be the most blessed thing you can nurture. Dance for us, and we will dance with you.

Be well, my sweet ones, for I hear the voices of children calling out in joy, and I must hear them with my love. Be blessed.

Haniel

***

July 3, 2014

Well, my training right now is to reach a higher vibration than my usual level. Gabriel is teaching me this. He decided that I should reach this level and didn't tell me what was at the other end.

Should have known—Gabriel and his surprises!

At Gabriel's request, I went into meditation mode. Through the tunnel that I use to go into a deep state, what I found at the other end was this charming small cottage with a beautiful interior. I approached it and opened the door. I walked through it and found that nearby was a long outside foyer that led to a stone building.

Gabriel told me this cottage was for me to use whenever I came to that higher level. Then he told me that I was to see how long I could keep up the higher vibration; I should not release it until he told me to stop and release.

> Sunday: 15 minutes
> Monday: 2 hours.
> Tuesday: 5 hours.
> Wednesday: got too busy and had a lot of distractions
> Today: tuned in at 5 a.m. and am still there

This gives me a slight sensation of being slightly off-centre in my mind but still functional. I close my eyes and am in the cottage. Sometimes the images get superimposed on each other if my eyes are open.

****

July 4, 2014

I have both Gabriel and Uriel here, but this is a message from Uriel.

What a wonderful world, beautiful in my sight. Your cities are like stars on the surface when seen from above. You too flicker with your own light and in all different colours. I think we should rename our lightworkers, Gabriel. Let us call them our rainbow children. After all, are they not all colours of the rainbow and more, physically and spiritually? They also shine like stars.

Everyone, you are our children, our rainbow children. Alike yet so different. But it is that difference that makes you all individually special to us. Each is a distinct personality.
But what makes you alike also is your feelings of laughter, joy, sadness, and love for love. Your art is similar yet individual. Your music is similar yet individual. See what I mean? You are all the same yet different. You are all special to us in your inner beauty and love light. You're special in that you are wonderful. You're special in that you are unique in every little way. You're special because you are made of the Divine's love. You are special, and we love that within you.

Let us enjoy your laughter with us, share your love and joy. We too take pleasure in each one of you.

Oh, such beauty and such love. I can do wonders with all this, and I enjoy helping you.

The many wonders that make you all are all down to one thing: the Divine. You were made by the Divine, we love the Divine, and we love you. We too are made by the Divine, and we know you love the Divine and us. We are all part of each other. Hence you are named to be our children. We are in a way part of the One. Hmm! Spiritually related, you could say. Well, we do share the same father, so I shall say we are spiritual siblings. Yet there is enough diversity to make you part of a different world.

I will introduce myself. I am Uriel, and I am the one who will light up your path to the Divine. I am the one who will lead you to the right path of life and destiny for you. I am the one who will watch over you and help to ease your trials in life. I am the one who loves you.

Be well, my sweet rainbow children. Let your soul shine like the stars they are, and let me enjoy the varied colours that they bring.

Be blessed, and you are.

Uriel

***

July 6, 2014

A message from Cassiel, and it's lovely.

>Welcome to my world.
>Welcome to your world.
>Welcome to our world.
>Yes! Our world.
>
>You who live in this world share it with us. We share this world with you too. We share each other in that our love is mutual. We all love the Divine, and the Divine loves us. Let us be happy in that, for there is nothing more precious and priceless as that love. It is healing, nurturing, and embracing. It is all that and more. That is what makes it priceless.
>
>We are surrounded by it, yet it is worth more than any jewel in your world. Let us revel in this love. I wish this love to be absorbed by you and surrounding you, just like we absorb it and it surrounds us. It is something we all want and need. Let us wrap ourselves in this mutual love for ourselves and each other.
>
>It is beautiful. You are beautiful.
>
>You are beautiful in the Divine's eyes; you are beautiful in ours. Oh, so beautiful! Your very life essence is like a brilliant spark that lights up the night. And when you all move and experience

various emotions, it changes colour. It is that essence that is your spiritual self, your soul. You are like the stars; you are the stars in your world. Gleaming, changing, and yet so strong in love and life. My sweet ones, never let that love die within you, for it is the very basis of your existence. You are made of Divine love, like we are.

My aim for you is to grow into the light. As you do so, you will find many doors opening into new paths. These paths that lead you to a wonderful, great future. This future will help you evolve. This in turn will bring you closer to the Divine light even more.

Do you know what it is like to be touched by the Divine? It is amazing. To be touched is to be blessed. It is to be accepted and loved. That touch is the new beginnings of a wonderful future. The touch is the final act of ascension. Those of you who have been touched will grow beyond what is in your world. They fulfil the greatest task of all on your world.

Jesus was one who had been touched.
Mother Theresa was another.
Yes, Buddha also ascended.

There are so many who have gained this touch, and they do the greatest and most selfless thing in your world: they give of themselves to others in the name of Divine love, so that the Divine love flourishes within others. That is a path of the ultimate sacrifice: the sacrifice of self so that they can work in the service of the Divine. They are the most blessed of all, and we treasure those ascended ones. This is the ultimate gift of all, and it is all for you to aim for.

I am Cassiel, and this I relate to you so that you may learn, love, and live without ego.

Be blessed, my children; I await your answer.

Cassiel

***

July 6, 2014

Daily Message from the Angels

Be blessed in what you can do. Even though your task may be menial and small, it is still a thing to be treasured. There are those who would love your work and are unable to do it due to some health issue.

Relish the thought that you can do what you do and do it well. Give healing love to those who are unable. Be strong for them so that they can be strong for you. After all, you may be surprised by what these people can do for you; perhaps it's something that you can't do yourself.

We are all equal in the eyes of the Divine, and we are all loved. In the Divine's eyes, the rich man sits beside the poor man, no different from each other.

Be well, beloved ones.

Gabriel

***

July 6, 2014

Update time.

I went into meditation mode again and found Uriel in front of me. Uriel told me to come with him, and we both walked to a hill with a tall tree on it. It was night there, and we both sat under the tree, relaxing; it was a magnificent view of the night sky.

Uriel told me that I'm very close to my next step, but I now need to master keeping up a protective shield around me for a long time—in fact, it was to be permanent. Once that is mastered, then events will start to move forward.

When the time came for us both to leave, Uriel came up to me and gave me a hug and a kiss on the forehead. Uriel stated that the friendship between Gabriel and me was a good bond, and that they all loved me.

We came back. By then I was starting to show signs of nodding off, and so Uriel said, "You're starting to drift away." This roused me back into meditation mode. He humorously told me to come back to earth.

Earlier on, I had prepared myself to do the daily message. I was just getting ready to tune in when I saw Gabriel standing nearby, grinning. Gabriel started to sing "Money Makes the World Go Around" and began hamming up the gestures for it.

I was in tears of laughter, and my vibrations heightened. I'm still chuckling over it. I must admit the angels love to clown about if it provides pure, honest laughter for everyone. I love these guys!

***

July 7, 2014

Daily Message from the Angels

Beloved ones, you are what I said you are: beloved.

You have the gifts of the universe at your fingertips, and you can do anything you can put your minds to. All you need to do is open your hands and hearts to receive them. They are yours to keep and show off. You already know of one gift and use it well: love. There is another you also use: laughter. There are more to come, and they are never ending.

Please stretch out your hands to us, and we will place them within your reach.

Let the gifts of the light be the gifts of your heart.

Let it be so.

Uriel

***

July 8, 2014

Daily Message from the Angels:

Have you ever experienced the stillness of thought? Meditation is the best way to experience that. Just sit there and clear your mind gradually.

I know that your mind keeps thinking no matter how much you try to clear it. That is normal. As your mind flicks a thought to you, acknowledge the thought, and it will settle down. Do this with each thought that flicks through your mind. Soon those thoughts will settle down, and you will enjoy your serene meditation. Don't try to smother the thoughts, or they will come back stronger. Simply let them come through, have a quick look at them, and then let it go.

That's all you need to do.

That is a way you can use if you have difficulties in this.

Raziel

***

July 8, 2014

I'm a bit drained of energy and tired. The angels were keeping their distance from me, but I found out it was the protective barrier that I had put around me to practice on that was muffling their communications with me. Seemingly the more tired I get, the harder it is for me to pick them up. The barrier didn't help. The barrier is down for the moment, and Azrael has decided to download energy into me to pep me up a bit. He's a good friend to have around.

During my daily message, Raziel told me I'm not to do any big messages for today; I'm to rest. He even held my hands down before and after the daily message. This tells me to finish off what I'm doing and rest. I agree, and how! So, no readings.

I've been told that they are also keeping their distance to give me some time with my own thoughts. They give me some space, in other words. I've been taking advantage of it to get to know my guardian angels better. Darryl has been helping me in checking my barrier by indicating if I missed a space.

Raziel did say that tomorrow could be another matter, energy wise. I assume that I can do my usual stuff then.

I'm feeling a hand on my head. I checked with Azrael, and he doesn't want to pass a message on. He's told me he's only downloading.

Ah, rest! My bed is making tempting messages at me. It must want me to give the pillow some head, and my mattress some ass. Ah, I thought that would make Azrael laugh. "Like it!" just flicked through my head.

***

July 9, 2014

Daily Message from the Angels

Go out into your world, go to the nearest hill or mound.
Look to the distance and see what the scenery is like.
Is it not beautiful?

Indeed, it is.

Now we look at your world. We stand here and see every detail.

You are our scenery.
You are our world.
You are precious to us.

We see how beautiful you are.

Don't put yourselves down by saying that you have spots, or your hair is a mess.
Don't say the scars you have are ugly.
To us, they are not. They are all part of you, and you are beautiful.

Never hide from us, because you can't. We can see you wherever you go, and we can see you too. You see, we are the experts. We do know the truth. And to us, you are truly the most beautiful thing that has ever been created.

Be well, sweet ones.

Haniel

***

July 9, 2014

Oh, my! I've just been visited by Michael again. We spoke briefly about protection and barriers—when to use them and how. Then he said to me that I'm very close to the next step—so close that I may as well take that step to go forward.

I went into deeper meditation, and this is what I experienced.

I saw a human figure made of white light appear in front of me, which began to rotate and merge with my body. I began to fly upwards into the sky. I began to expand with energy, which in turn started to swirl around me until I was surrounded by the light. I kept heading upwards. During this moment in time, I began to shake physically.

Soon I found myself soaring through another universe, not ours. I saw strange lights. As I continued my upwards journey, I began to see angels fly towards me and then join me at my side. The entire time I heard Michael repeating, "Keep going! Keep going!"

Within a short moment, we stopped, and as my vision cleared, I noticed that I was in this room made of light. The walls were all around me and glowed blue-white.

I felt relaxed and my hands hung down at my sides, yet I felt as if there was some weight around or on my shoulders.

Michael and another Angel stood on either side of me, and we walked forward. Michael took a few more steps ahead, stood in front of me, and turned to face me. He put a hand on my forehead and said, "Your vibrational levels are high enough for me to do this with ease." A surge of energy shot through his hand and into my forehead. Strange memories and energy shot through me. I began to physically spasm in my seat. I could feel the vibrations in my meditation state.

Still his hand rested on my forehead, pouring energy into me. There was another hand on the right side of my head, which kept it steady. I think it was the other angel who placed his hand there.

The energy began to ease off, and I found myself being pulled back into my body.

I'm now sitting here in my chair, feeling like there is a tight band around my head, as well as a slight feeling of drunkenness even though I don't drink alcohol. The pressure around and on my head tells me that I'm starting to do a large download again. Here we go again!

A headache that had started before this meditation has now gone up a couple of notches. This only happens when I go up a level. What it did to me is too soon to tell, but I'll keep you posted.

***

July 10, 2014

Did some drawing today. I refrained from asking whom I was drawing until I finished it, which is what I normally do. I was working with my art guide, Mike, when I drew this. It is Jophiel.

***

July 11, 2014

Daily Message from the Angels

If someone offers you a hug, accept! Hug back!
If someone offers you wise words, accept! Thank them.
If someone offers you unconditional love and friendship, accept and return the gift back!

Yes, love is the only gift in this world that you can return to the sender. There is nothing physical about it, but it is there for you to work with. Return the gift of love, and remember to share it with others so that they too can return that gift to you.

Now, isn't that wonderful?

Chamuel

***

July 12, 2014

Daily Message from the Angels

Let go of that which does not serve you, for it will stop you from going forward. Leave those who try to put you down, for they are weak and envy your strength. Remove those who are aggressive towards you, for they have no control and wish to control you.

See the pattern.

All these are negative energies which you do not need. They will harm you by holding you back and dragging you down to the black hole of depression or self-destruction. You need to face the light and walk forward. That is the way of growth, confidence, and self-power.

And let it be known that no matter which direction you step into, we still love you. Even though it saddens us, who see those who chose the path of self-destruction.

Remember that we all love and watch over you.

Be with love, my sweet ones.

Muriel

***

July 13, 2014

Daily Message from the Angels

Well, it is that time. The time to reflect on what you have done with your life.

If you have helped someone in your past who needed that help, well done!

If you have listened to someone who was lonely, well done!

If you have played with a child despite being very busy, well done!

Have you laughed with joy during a moment of sadness within you, well done indeed!

But if you rejected an offer for help that you really did need? No matter; you have learned something. If you have refused to aid someone in trouble? No matter; you have learned something. If you have cried when others are having fun? No matter; you have learned something.

You see, it's all about choices and what you make of them. No matter how bad the choice is, it is all part of your learning path. Learn well. Be assured that we haven't stopped looking after you and giving you our love. You are here in this world to learn something, and by your choices, you are learning.

Be at peace within yourself; all are meant to be so within you.

Be blessed, my beloved ones.

Haniel

***

July 13, 2014

Message from Archangel Chamuel

Beloved ones, I come to you to pass on my message and my love. Yes, you!

My message is that you need to love each other more. You must learn that the path to enlightenment is the path of love.

Let us start with yourself first. Look in the mirror. What do you see?

As you are looking at yourself, state out loud what you love about yourself. Yes, I understand it is hard, but it is so easy.

As you are looking in the mirror, tell yourself that you are perfect in every way. Say you are perfection in the eyes of the Divine and in the eyes of the angels—which you are. You really are perfect to us.

Even acknowledge that your soul is perfection also. For it is! For you to have a perfect soul, you must be perfect. And as your soul is perfect, then you are perfect too. Yes, you are all perfect right now and forever. Trust me on this.

Now, every time you see yourself, say how perfect you are and how you love yourself. Say it out loud. Mind you, don't say it in public, or you will get strange looks. Say it in your mind. As you say all of this, most important, believe it! That's right. Believe in what you are saying and believe in yourself.

Once you have this instilled in your mind about how perfect you are and how much you love yourself as you are, you will find yourself becoming stronger and more confident. It is a real booster to the spirit.

When all this is done to yourself, turn to the nearest human beings and give them a hug. Tell them that you love them for being alive, for being themselves, or for just love's sake. You decide. You can even create another reason to hug or love these people. If the love is shared, you can work wonders.

Ah, yes, there are some people with whom you daren't do that, so I've been told. I understand! With those people, simply send your love via thought and smile.

All is part of love.

If the people are too far away to receive your love physically, sending loving thoughts to them is just as good. You have guides who can deliver that love to those people. That is what some of your guides can do for you. It is their job, and they do it because they love you too.

No matter who you love or who loves you, love is universal and never-ending. You can get your fill of it whenever you want and wherever you want. It is free. It is around you, and it is within you.

Well, my perfect, beautiful ones, get out there and spread the love, and spread the message of love.

I leave you now with this thought.

Chamuel

***

July 14, 2014

Daily Message from the Angels

Be aware of what is around you, for our answers come in many forms and in many directions. You may not see the sudden movement of a bird leading you to the right direction, or the flutter of a butterfly as it tries to catch your eye into a certain spot. Keep an eye open, because we are determined that your questions be answered. And we will answer them in subtle and varied ways.

Be well, my loves,

Barachiel

***

July 15, 2014

Daily Message from the Angels

Do you ever stop still, listen to the silence, and become aware of your inner beat? Not your heartbeat but the beat in your soul. Do you then listen to that beat within and move your inner self to its rhythm?

That beat is the sound of your spiritual energy pulsating through your inner self. It pulsates through you, energizing and sustaining your aura. It is the beat of love and life. You are part of that beat, so you can dance with it. In doing so, you will find yourself vibrating with that energy at a higher level. And you are all so beautiful when you do that.

Dance with love.

Meriel

Meriel is not an archangel but a healing angel. Meriel my teacher for healing and is good fun to work with. I love Meriel to bits.

***

July 16, 2014

I once had a vision of me in a blue room, but I was wearing a long dove-grey cloak over my shoulders.

Now, normally I would bypass it as part of the vision, but lately the cloak and its colour have been getting to me. I had even felt the weight of the cloak.

***

July 16, 2014

Daily Message from the Angels

Be blessed! Yes, you are.

Your days are watched over by us as we wait for your next step in life, but better still, your nights are guarded by us so that you may be safer. As you sleep, we surround you in the energy of protection, healing, and light. This is protective, and we do keep a very close eye on you all during this time when you are most vulnerable, so we will watch over you.

Remember, you are protected by the light by day and by night. The light of protection is one of our gifts to you, and the Divine has told us to give this gift to you all freely. And we do, and we do this willingly.

Be safe, my beloved ones. We will watch over you when you sleep.

Chamuel

***

July 18, 2014

Daily Message from the Angels

I'd better let you know that I didn't know who I was channelling until after the message. I asked for the name twice for confirmation and got it. The words "I love you" were whispered in my ear, and then I found myself crying. I'm still a bit weepy. This is the first time I've ever channelled one of the ascended ones.

> It is the best for you that we watch over you during times of stress. We watch and wait for you to call us to help you. We wait and always wait for you. Call us; we come in an instant. Sing to us; we hear it from your heart. Dance to us; we dance with you.
>
> Oh, so many ways we interact with you all and on many levels. Laugh, and we laugh, so don't be afraid to joke with us. We enjoy it. Be aware that we are always aware and watching over you. You are the most precious treasure in the Divine's light. You are the future of your world, and we are your teachers to be.
>
> Some of you are of my children.
>
> Shine on, my sweet ones; you are our promise, the Divine's promise, and the universal promise.
>
> Be well, my loved ones.
>
> Mary Magdalene

***

July 18, 2014

A message from Muriel, and it's beautiful.

> Do you have a song that brings such joy and happiness to you? A song which has a lot of meaning to you? I see a few of you are nodding your heads. Well, let that song touch the very innermost part of you, your spirit. Let the song play within. You will feel wonderful when you do so.
>
> If you sing out loud, we will sing with you. You may not hear us, but your spirit and higher self-will, and they will sing in harmony with us. Our song is that of light and love, of freedom and flight. They are the songs that will change your universe as you know it. We are the music within you, and we are the musicians that play your music of light. Let us play our music together and bring more light into this world.
>
> There is darkness in your world—we know of that. But we are very well aware that there is much more light than darkness in some places. That is because of the music of the light. We are also aware that there are places that have more darkness than light. The music is quiet and not sung in there.
>
> Yes, it is all out of balance.

You are our instruments, you are our voices, and you are our beloved ones. Sing with us, my friends. Let your voices soar across time and space so that the Divine will derive much pleasure from your songs. Sing of life and love, for they are eternal. Sing out loud, because you too are eternal. Let us sing together. Let us join united for this.

Beloved ones, never feel shame for singing out loud. Never! For it is a physical form of joy. And what brings joy to you brings joy to us. We derive pleasure from seeing you happy and laughing. It is what we want for you: happiness. Sing with all your heart and let the joy shine out of your eyes and your voice.

What more do we need? Only your love. That is a small price, and it is never-ending. Please love, sing, and be happy. In return we will send you love, sing with you, and be happy for you. All is well in the song of universal love. That is the song that is within you, and your body resounds with it. Even the smallest of infants know of this song.

Be blessed, my beloved ones. You have become more than what you were before. Changes have come upon several of you, and they have shown themselves in miraculous ways. Our mediums have changed levels and are stronger. Even those who claim to have no abilities have grown—yes, those who deny they have any gifts in a spiritual way.

Well, you are wrong. You all have gifts.

The gift of love is a most wondrous gift. Share it. The gift of laughter is another. Share it.

The gift of life—share it.
The gift of you: believe in yourself.

I shall leave you now with my words. Let it be known to you all that we love you all—every single one of you.

Be blessed.

Muriel

***

July 19, 2014

Daily Message from the Angels

There is something special about you all. That something special is called love. You are made of it, you are part of it, and you are filled with it. It is because we gave it to you willingly. It is all part and parcel of the essence within you called the Divine light. After all, the Divine gave this love to us to share with you. And of course, we added some of our own love too.

Please accept this gift of love with more love within you, just like I accept your love and return it back to you. Please raise your hands and prepare to accept this Divine gift.

I love you all.

Jeremiel

***

July 19, 2014

A little something happened yesterday.

I was busy doing my guardian angel introductions when I felt that there was a presence sitting to the right of me. I quickly checked with my Spidey senses and found one of the archangels sitting beside me.

I didn't recognise this one, and it appeared to be looking in the middle distance and away from me. It looked as if it was sitting on a chair and was reclining in it, one leg crossed over the other. It had long, straight whitish hair and slim build. It was approximately ten to twelve feet tall with long, slim fingers, and it wore cream clothing.

I felt that it was watching other things unfolding in other parts of the world but had one sense open towards me. A flicker of an eye towards me and a quick smile appeared when it saw I had noticed it. As I said, I didn't recognise this angel.

I asked my guardian angel for a clue, and the name Barachiel came to me.

I said the name out loud, and Barachiel's voice came to me, acknowledging that I got the name right. It told me that it was visiting me so that I got to know it better and added that it was watching over me that night. I greeted Barachiel and thanked it for visiting me.

Now I know what Barachiel looks like.

***

July 20, 2014

Daily Message from the Angels

Let the gentle silence of the night embrace you during your sleep. Let it enfold you in its blanket of peace.

Sleep is the time for your soul to start learning new things, the time for exploring without the hindrance of dragging a fleshly body with it. Your soul flies freely during this phase, searching from place to place, looking for answers, visiting friends, and even helping other souls who have passed on but are lost.

Never take your sleep for granted, for even then you are a very busy person. It is your spirit's time to be free, and your body's time to rest.

Well, you could say fly by night.

Be well, and sorry for the joke.

    Gabriel

Gabriel, that was a terrible joke! You're a shocker! I can't stop laughing now. You're not one bit sorry about that joke.

***

July 21, 2014

Daily Message from the Angels

Look around you and see your world in all its natural beauty. Even in the city, there does nature reign. Nature is everywhere. Nature is within you all and with you. You can't hide from it, for you are part of nature too.

A bird singing, a butterfly on a flower, wind in the trees, even the sunshine on the grass—that is nature. The rain that runs down a window pane, the humble and strong sparrow stealing crumbs, even a humble beetle skittering across a concrete block—that is nature.

No matter what you do to your world, nature is always there and will never be removed. Instead of trying to hide or destroy it, be one with it. The benefits are bountiful to you.

Be with nature and love, sweet ones.

Ariel

***

July 21, 2014

This morning while I was watching Sky TV, I decided to see what spirits were with me.

I knew my guides and guardian angels were around me, and so I asked whether I was alone with them only and got a no. Curious, I asked whether it was Meriel (my healing angel and guide) and was told no again. This time I asked whether it was another angel and got a yes. It was like extracting teeth!

I decided to find out who it was that was with me. I put forth my Spidey senses and felt a presence a bit behind me and to the left. I sensed amusement and love. The name Ariel came to my mind, and I confirmed it with my visitor. I sensed Ariel come up behind me and gently place her hands on my arms, and I had a feeling of being wrapped in something.

We had a quick chat, and I felt Ariel stroke my cheek. Ariel had come to visit and keep an eye on me, as well as to let me get to know her better.

Ariel wanted to let me know that she wanted to do the daily message.

I've got her support in the next stage of my destiny.

***

July 22, 2014

Daily Message from the Angels

Beloved ones, do you not see the wonders of the Divine? Do you not see the beauty that is in your world? Please stop what you are doing, and I will show you the perfect thing in this world of yours.

Go to a full-length mirror and look at yourself.

That is right! You are the perfect thing in this world. You are part of the beauty and wonder in your world. Be assured that in the Divine's eyes and in ours; you are perfection. What more do you want? You are perfect for the life you have chosen. You are perfect for this world. And you are perfect to us.

Be blessed, my lovely ones.

Michael

***

July 23, 2014

Daily Message from the Angels

There are many forms of lightworkers in your world. I shall name a few of them.

Beacons: They bear the light up to all so that those who are lost can find their way.

Lightwarriors: They will defend those who are weak or defenceless, all in the name of love, compassion, and the Divine.

Lightsingers: Their voices call to the Divine in song. They can lift the vibrations by voice alone. Those who listen to them will have their vibrations also lifted. This is a gift from the Divine.

Messengers: They pass on the words of us angels and the Divine. Their messages from us are to you all. They are also known as the heralds.

Wisdoms: They are the teachers. They take in the less-skilled lightworkers and train them so that they grow and develop to higher levels. They are also the advisers. Some messengers can take this role.

Lightseekers: They search out those who are lost in the darkness, are unable to see the light, but are willing to be turned to the light. The lightseekers are the rescue workers of the lightworkers. They also work hand in hand with the lightwarriors.

You see, this is some of the most important of the lightworkers. There are more: the scribes and the healers.

Scribes: They record the word of the Divine. They record our words. Scribes also double as messengers if they so wish.

Healers: They come under Raphael and are solely run by Raphael. Those who are "damaged" by the darkness can be healed by the healers. They are also healing the world with a thought and energy.

Yes, there are more, but this is not the time for their mention. I don't wish to confuse you, so I shall leave them for later: the guiding lights, the joybringers, and the heavenly ones. They are a different level indeed, higher.

You have your starting points, and you might recognise yourself in some of them. Which one do you think you are? I shall leave you with this knowledge, dear ones.

I thank you all.

Gabriel

***

July 24, 2014

Daily Message from the Angels

There is much in this world to be thankful of.
Be thankful for the sun, the stars, the trees, and the flowers.
Be thankful for the birds, the animals, and the bees.
Be thankful for the love you have for each other and be thankful that the Divine loves you.
Above all, be thankful for being yourselves. Are you not bathed in the light?

Yes, you who read this know you are. For you are drawn to this message. And this message is to confirm that you are loved by all of us. We also love those who don't read this, but they will never realise our love for them because they can't be told.

It is up to you, my lightworkers, to show them that they are loved—and that they will be loved even more if they let peace and love rule their lives.

Let there be peace in this world. Let there be harmony. For in order for your world to grow, such is needed within all of you.

Be well and in peace.

Haniel

***

July 25, 2014

A message from Chamuel.

Let us try something out, my lovely ones. It will be fun, I promise. You don't have to back out with uncertainty or fear.

Let us try this.

Think of the most wonderful day you have ever experienced in your life. The day that made your heart sing and your entire body tingle with excitement.

Notice how you felt about that day. You felt wonderful then, and with this memory, you are feeling wonderful now. That feeling is what I am going to bring to your attention. That feeling has increased your vibrations to us. And in doing so, you are letting in more of the Divine light.

This is also good for you. Enjoy it.

Relish the feeling of the light enveloping your wonderful memory. Feel the light absorb into your body. It is healing and refreshing, and it heightens that wonderful memory. Yes, now that memory will become even more special, for that wonderful thought has been blessed with the light. Keep the memory close to your heart; it is, after all, yours only, and it is a beautiful event that happened to you. It has been worth every bit of it.

That feeling of excitement, joy, and love is what we want you to feel all the time. It is part of the light and part of you. Never feel embarrassed for enjoying such fine memories. Don't let anyone stop you by telling you that you can't live in the past. You know fine well you can't, but the good memories of that time are for you to recall, enjoy, and savour. They are your memories, not theirs. Enjoy them as they are free. And in them, you are free.

Be blessed in having such thoughts and recall. We want you to enjoy your best moments and remember them. They are precious you and to us.

Such good memories are a type of love. Now, isn't that a good thing? Without memories, you'd never learn anything. You would be like the rocks in the mountains or the sand in the deserts. You would not be aware, and you would not see the light. That is one state of mind I do not relish, for it means extinction.

I want you all to protect your thoughts, yourselves, and each other. Alone you stand tall, but you stand apart from the rest, left behind and lonely. Be with a group of those who are like-minded as you are, and you will find strength in each other's love. That strength will protect you from those who want to hurt you.

Let love guide you to these people. They are the lightworkers. Let us guide you.

Be well, my beloved friends, and thank you, my messenger.

Chamuel

***

July 25, 2014

Daily Message from the Angels

Let it be so, my friends.

When the world seems to block the path, you want to go on. Let it be so, for it means that you aren't destined to go that way. Your path is in another direction.

When others shun you, let it be so. It means you aren't meant to be with that person. You belong with someone better.

At times you find it hard to carry on. Let it be so. It is a time of learning, and when you have learned enough, you will find things will improve.

When tears threaten to pour, let it be so. It is cleansing. The tears will remove the negative energies that are temporarily surrounding you. These too will pass.

When you feel angry but daren't release, let it be so. Redirect it in a more positive direction. That way, it won't fester within you but will instead strengthen you.

Above all, when any of these situations happen and you have difficulties, call upon me. I am Azrael, and

I can give you the strength and calmness to get you through the worst.

This I can do for you.

Be blessed, sweet ones.

Azrael

***

July 26, 2014

Daily Message from the Angels

As the season changes to another, from you there is a requirement. You need to observe them, see what is affected by the changes, and learn. You need to learn this so that you can adapt and change with the seasons. As you change with the seasons, you will change over the years. As the trees change with each passing season, so will you. Both tree and you will grow.

The change is gradual, yet it comes so fast. Change with the passing of time and do it with grace. Don't complain and dig in your heels, for that means you will be left behind, all alone. Change, accept what comes with time, and grow with it. You will never regret it, and your spirit will grow. It is all worth it in the end, and the growth means you will shine brighter with the light of Divine love.

I thank you, my blessed ones.

Gabriel

***

July 27, 2014

Daily Message from the Angels

Beloved ones, are you ready to take the next step in your greatest adventure of all times? Will you stand up and out, showing the world that you are the perfection we all are? Will you be that example?

Yes, it is time!

Time for you to stand up and be counted.

Time for you to rise and show off your special strengths and abilities.

Time for you to surround your world with Divine love and light.

Things are happening, and it is amazing. You are the lightworker who will know of this first. This is your time to shine and show off your abilities. Yes, it is that time.

The time is that of enlightenment. It is the turn of the lightworkers to bring it all to you, to direct and show you.

Are you willing to show the world that you are precious and perfect, that you are a product of Divine love?

Be well, my sweet ones. You are all coming into your own.

Uriel

***

July 28, 2014

Daily Message from the Angels

Believe in yourselves always! For you are all physical embodiment of the Divine will. The Divine believes in you, and so you are quite safe in believing in yourselves.

Never shy away from opportunities that will happen before you, fearing ridicule or retribution. That is not what that opportunity is for. Instead, it is for growth, love, and above all you! The Divine will within you wants you to go forward with that opportunity, so don't hold it back. To do so is to deny the Divine gift that is given to you.

Please shine your Divine will like a light and step forward into your destiny—your destiny of eternal Divine love, your destiny of bountiful future, your destiny that is wonderful. Take the opportunity before you as they appear and don't look back. It is for you alone.

Grow, my children.

I believe in you.

Azrael

***

July 28, 2014

A little bit of info from me.

The angels have a rather mischievous sense of humour. In fact, they are the biggest pranksters. The worst offender is Archangel Michael. I sense a few archangels are laughing at this. I see Michael raising his hands and looking upwards in an "I admit it!" gesture.

Well, the best way to deal with their pranks is to do the same back at them, tease them. They play their jokes on me, and I do the same thing back because my sense of humour is equally twisted.

Enjoy the fun, and you will find that they will have you laughing. Your vibrations will rise higher with the fun. Yes, Michael is smiling at this and nodding.

Be prepared to be teased, Michael. His words: "You wish! Bring it on, beloved!"

***

July 29, 2014

Daily Message from the Angels

Walk away from conflict, for that path is not for you.
Walk away from those who hurt you. You do not need them.
Walk away from problems that are lumbered onto you. It's not your problem; it's theirs.
Walk away from those who would pull you down. You are better than them.
Walk away from the darkness. The flower that is you will bloom better in the Light.
Walk away from danger, because you are precious to others.
Walk away from hate. It will damage you.

But walk towards the light; it will bring you much love.
Walk towards your child, because the child wants you as you are.
Walk towards those who love you. You are the most important thing in the world to them.
Walk towards those who help you, as like attracts like.
Walk towards peace. It is uplifting and growing.
Walk towards the Divine, and we will help you on your path.

Michael

***

July 30, 2014

Daily Message from the Angels

Be true to your own self. You are the one who must live with yourself for the rest of your life, so don't let anyone force you to do things that you feel are wrong. You are the one who is special to us, and we feel sad when one is corrupted by another person. We must work hard at trying to bring that person forward and up, but it doesn't work when that person doesn't listen to us.

So please be true.

It is not hard to remain true. Believe in yourself. Love yourself and rise above all those who would try to harm you. Walk away from them or banish them from your life. Believe that you are made of love, created by the Divine, and therefore perfect in every way.

You are beautiful.
You are smart.
You are wonderful.

Tell yourself that and believe in it. You are all that and more! There is nothing more beautiful and perfect than you yourself. Isn't that wonderful in its own right? We think so. Please enjoy it.

We love you.

Gabriel

***

July 30, 2014

Something happened this morning.

I was informed that I was the one blocking my ability to see spirit. This intrigued me, and so I asked some questions. One of my guides confirmed that I was blocking myself, and it was due to the fact I was not interacting with my guides very much.

After a bit of talking with my guides, I said I would like to unblock myself but didn't know how or where to start. I asked if it would it be OK if someone could help me with this. It was confirmed.

I asked out and Archangel Azrael appeared. He told me that I always had the ability, and Michael had enhanced it, but it needed reactivating. He also informed me that it was that lack of use that was making me one-sided, and that Michael had told me to grow outwards. The outwards part was the awakening of my spiritual medium side. It was to be opened again. I was also told that it was where my guides would help me the most, so I must contact them more often. Azrael said that I needed to lay rules.

On hearing this, I told my guides that I was willing to reopen that side of my abilities. I told my guide Andricus (my doorkeeper) that he was to let in those who weren't negative; he was to vet them for me. He should let them in one at a time, and he was to tell me when to stop when he thought I've had enough. Andricus agreed.

My main contact guides were to keep those spirits who had negative energies away from me. They were to protect me if things went wrong. They agreed.

Ben (my messenger guide) would help in blocking out the negative ones' words, and he'd help me see. Mike (my art guide) would help me provide images if I was drawing. Veyna (my music guide) admitted she couldn't help much, but she would help in protection as much as she could.

After this, I turned to Azrael, who was still listening in. He approved what rules I had made and then reached over and put his finger into my third eye. I felt a probing sensation in my third eye. I closed my eyes and waited for it to ease. A couple of minutes later, I opened them and saw that my vision was a bit off.

Azrael told me to meditate, and instead of rising higher to the angelic realm, I was to go deep within myself. I did this and soon was visited by a spirit who stood in front of me. He gave me his name as Marco D'Allegini and said that Azrael had told him to come so that I may practice.

We got to talking. Marco had the features of an old man. I found that he came from Verona, Italy, in the eighteenth century and was of minor aristocracy. He was a son of a lord but was not the heir. He showed me the apple orchard he had, where he'd played as a child.

Marco came close to me, and I began to feel sadness and tears form in my eyes. I told him to stand back because I was feeling his emotions. Marco told me that that was another rule I needed to make.

I told my main contact guide, Amaru, that no spirits were to get close to me due to my feeling their grief or pain unless I specifically asked them to come near. It was agreed.

Now prepared, I reached forward with my spirit hands and held Marco's hands. Marco appeared surprised at the touch; he told me that the ability to control my spirit hands was a gift. I would able to touch and feel spirits with them. Soon he indicated he had to leave.

Marco looked up at the sky, a white light shone on him, and he rose up to meet it.

Azrael then came through and told me Marco was helping me in learning. Azrael asked me to come with him, and I found myself sinking deeper into a dark tunnel. I was wary, but he said that I was safe while he was around me.

Soon I reached a cavern within this tunnel, and in the middle was another angel. This one was very tall. This angel had such an air of power about them. It reached forward and picked me up, holding me gently in its arms. This angel then told me that its name was Seraphiel and that it was going to help me in this.

It pointed to another angel in the corner and told me this new angel was called Zaphriel. Zaphriel had taken on a male form. It said that Zaphriel was a fallen angel but was seeking redemption. Zaphriel was to look after me by keeping the dark spirits away from me, because otherwise they would harm me. That was all that Zaphriel was to do. I was also told that I wasn't to trust Zaphriel, and Zaphriel was indifferent to me. We both had our jobs to do, and Zaphriel would do his. His job was to keep the darkness away and no more. We would rarely interact with each other unless necessary. Zaphriel did not hate me, but he didn't love me either.

Seraphiel mentioned that they would be watching over Zaphriel, checking up and making sure nothing happened to me. Zaphriel was to act as a bodyguard for my spirit. That was his task for redemption.

I was then told to go back.

As soon as I got to my body, I asked Azrael about Zaphriel. I was told again to not trust him. I was told that Seraphiel and Azrael would keep an eye on things. Azrael told me that he would help me and teach me on this. He had been waiting for quite a while for me to make the first move.

Michael then came through and confirmed it all, adding that this was what he was waiting for too.

I opened my eyes and found that my mind felt off-centre, and that I was starting a big headache in the third-eye region. Azrael appeared amused at this and told me that I was very close to the next step of ascension. I was also told that spirit talking would trigger off that. He informed me that I may or may not notice it if my mind was occupied, but I would know the effects. He told me that not every step had the same effects or visions; some were subtle.

Several hours later, I still feel the same. I have been told by Azrael that I can talk with Zaphriel if I so wish.

I did so.

I felt his indifference and asked if he was doing this willingly. He confirmed it was so and that he would look after me because he wanted his redemption. He had made a mistake and was willing to work his way back. That was when I replied that I hoped he got his redemption. As soon as I said that; I felt his indifference change to sadness and relief. He began to cry, to my amazement.

I asked why he was crying. He said it was because I was the only one who cared at this level. It appears that I was the first human who hadn't judged or rejected him. He backed off.

I began to feel a small trickle of thought enter my mind that came from Azrael, stating that I had just made an ally in Zaphriel. He would be even more diligent in protecting me now. If Zaphriel started to love me as the other angels did, then it would help him in his redemption even more.

Damn it! It was a test for me!

Wheels within wheels, circles within circles, time within time—all are within each other. Beginnings and endings. But what is the beginning, and what is the end? Or is it all the same?

***

July 31, 2014

Another daily message from the angels, with Chamuel's typical humour.

>Well, hello, everyone. Yes, I greet you all, just like you must greet everyone you meet with a smile. Even if that person is what you think of as a grumpy bugger. Yes, them too.
>
>Always greet the grump with a big smile and your eyes full of affection. It has excellent effects on that person in time. The stone within that one will start to crack, and a tentative smile will start to form. Keep on smiling at that person, but not to the extent of looking manic.
>
>You want to person to give you affection back, not scare them.
>
>When that stone breaks from that person's heart, the light of love will start to warm and grow. And what better way than to give friendship willingly and without conditions Does it not say, "Love thy neighbour, as much as you would love yourself"?
>
>That is how the Divine light grows within one's heart.
>
>Be with love.
>
>Chamuel

***

August 1, 2014

Daily Message from the Angels

Peace be upon you all. It is much needed for you and your world. Enough with the wars and the pain. Enough with sadness and grief. Instead, meditate!

All of you, please concentrate on world peace when you next meditate. Envision surrounding your world in pure white light energy. Fill that energy with love and peace. Ask the Divine and his angels to add their love and peace and spread this light around.

Ask for it to be so and that you want this to happen, and you want with your love and the Divine's blessings.

Let this be so and let the love flow into the heart of every single creature that walks, swims, and flies on your world.

Be blessed.

Seraphiel

***

August 2, 2014

Daily Message from the Angels

Aren't you all such wonderful people? You have the world in your hands, and yet the Divine has you in its hands. The Divine is your world, your sun, and your universe. You are the energy fields of life that circulate around the Divine.

And what is giving you the power to be part of the Divine's life force? The Divine itself. You are part of the Divine, and the Divine is part of you. We angels are part of the Divine too, and we are also part of you. Now you see we are all interconnected. Neither of us can exist without the love of the Divine holding us together.

The other names for the Divine are God, Goddess, Supreme Being, or the Light. So many names and so many aspects, yet all are the one being: The Divine. And all are the one energy: The Divine light.

So much to learn and so much to experience. That is the meaning of life. As you learn, the Divine experiences. This is how we all understand your world.

Be well and be at peace.

Muriel

***

August 2, 2014

I received a message from Chamuel.

> This is the time for personal growth: Time for the reason to evolve. You have felt the strange energies that have been flowing through you. You have seen their effects on you. This is the moment when you evolve. The energies are from us to you. This is the moment of the beginning of your new future. Embrace the change or be left behind.
>
> This is all for you.
>
> Many have taken these energies and are using them now as they are supposed to be used. Their abilities have grown stronger, more focused, and defined. Others have experienced this change and are trying to learn their new abilities. But some fear this change. It is these people we must educate. By *we* I mean us all—you and me. These energies are nothing to fear but are good, enlightening, and vibrant. Your energies have heightened to new levels, bringing you closer to us.
>
> You are all the next generation to start the new future. Not to be sneezed at, is it? For it is more than you ever believed.

My lightworkers, use these changes in your work. Learn to control and direct them. This energy is for all to use. Use it!

Love is the most powerful force in your world and in ours. In that we are united. Well, let those who fear this new energy understand that it is all pure love in an energy form. It can't harm you; it never will. You are safe with this energy of love, and you are safe with us. We would never let any harmful come near you. So be brave, test your new energies, and let it flow through you. Yes, you will feel the absolute love we feel for you. Grow with it and become one with it. You will become love in a physical form. All of you!

You are given this gift by the Divine. And we accept you as our gift from the Divine.

Beautiful ones, we are for each other. There is nothing stronger than the bond of love between you and us. That is what makes us all powerful.

Be blessed, my beautiful ones. Be true and be with love.

Chamuel

***

August 3, 2014

Daily Message from the Angels

Let love rule you, for you are the stars in the eyes of the Divine, and the Divine is love.

Let the light rule you, for you are the physical form of the Divine, and the Divine is the light.

Let joy rule you, for you were created with joy by the Divine, and the Divine gave joy to you.

Let the Divine rule you, for you are part of the Divine, and the Divine is part of you.

This is how it is meant to be.

Raphael

***

August 4, 2014

Daily Message from the Angels

Go forth and prosper in your life. Enjoy the fruits of the forest and of the harvest. Go forth and live the life you are supposed to have. This will be a life of happiness and joy. Aren't these things you were born to do? Aren't you supposed to live like that? Yes! You are meant to live your life to the fullest and enjoy every single moment of it. Remember, you make your own life choices, and you make your own happiness.

Whether you want to live in the light of love and laughter or live in sorrow and hardship, take note. It is your choice whether you want to live one way or another. It is also your choice to leave either. Your choice alone—not ours. We will never interfere with your free will and your choices. All we can do is try to make each path as easy as it can for you, and to send you our love. Your choice is yours alone. All we can say is be careful with what you wish for, for it may come true.

Trust, happiness, and being true to yourself. That is all you need to make that one perfect choice.

Be well,

Ariel

***

August 5, 2014

Daily Message from the Angels

Blessed be those who look to the light and see themselves there. For they see the perfection in themselves. They see the Divinity within.

Blessed be those who care for those in need. They are caring for themselves also. For as you see others in the light of the Divine, you will see yourselves in another aspect.

Treat others as you would like to be treated yourself, and you will be made aware of the sweet gentleness that is within you. This is one of the gifts that come from the Divine. This is the gift we would love to see you use more of.

Be aware of your inner light shining bright with the Divine's love for you.

Grow and be loved, my dearest ones.

Raphael

***

August 6, 2014

Daily Message from the Angels

Do you let in trouble to mess up your life? Why do you allow it? It should never be that way. Instead, block that negative energy and let in the light. The energy for good and harmony is shown as light. Let it in and let go of what is bringing you down. Your view on your own life will change. Things will suddenly seem brighter, music is sweeter, and perfect love will enter your life.

What could be better?

Love will attract love. The light will attract light. Sweetness will attract sweetness. And you will attract it all threefold. It is beautiful when that happens. Share the love, and love will be given back to you in triplicate.

Now, isn't that worthwhile?

Ariel

***

August 6, 2014

This is a picture of my now third guardian angel, Zaphriel. He's a fallen angel who is seeking redemption via me. He's got a rather wicked sense of humour, and we're getting on like a house on fire.

***

August 7, 2014

Ezekiel wanted to be my model for this one. When I first saw Ezekiel, I was amazed by its loving energy and big, beaming smile. Appears to be either North African to Egyptian in appearance. Ezekiel favours that look.

Every time I see Ezekiel, I find my face breaking out into a smile.

***

August 7, 2014

Daily Message from the Angels

Love, and be at peace within yourself, for then you will be at peace with others. That is a feeling that shows in your vibrations, and it shows in your heart. Such is soothing, and a mind at peace is a mind that is whole emotionally, spiritually and physically. You have reached your level of your soul's growth.

Peace as such is much-needed in meditation. You can only grow when it happens. If there is no peace in your life, how can you find it within your heart? You can't!

You must therefore remove all drama from your life. Remove the problems that aren't yours in the first place; they belong to the people who caused them. Let them deal with it. They need to learn from their own mistakes anyway. If there is an illness that is causing such stress, compassion and love will help to ease the pain in your heart. That is better for all. And don't forget to ask us to help in this situation.

Be at peace with yourself and grow. You will find that no problem is too big and that your heartache is replaced by love. Let it be so, dear ones.

Raphael

***

August 8, 2014

Daily Message from the Angels

Beloved ones, do you ever slow down and rest your eyes on a small flower, or at least a butterfly?

Even in such little things as a mere weed or an insect, there is such beauty. That beauty is called nature. Nature is beautiful, and you are part of nature. You can't run from her; you can't hide from her. You are very much a part of nature because you are part of the light.

Give in and enjoy the beauties of nature. It is free for all.

Gabriel

***

August 9, 2014

Daily Message from the Angels

Let those who love you enter your heart. Love is good and strong.
Let those who believe you enter your world. Friendship is mighty.
Let those who are your beloved blood and kin be joined with you. They will be your support.
Let those who are bonded to you be one with you. You can never have a better soul bond.
Let those who open to your words hear you. For they will make your words shine to others.
Let those who bring the light into your life; they will be your guardian angels.

Treasure them all, for they are all yours to love.

Be well.

Seraphiel

***

August 10, 2014

Daily Message from the Angels

Have you seen the sun in the sky? How it shines down upon you when you think you are lost? Notice that it always seems to shine when a time you feel saddened. Even when it is cloudy in the sky, the sun is still there, shining its light upon your world and you.

The Divine is like that. The Divine is always there. Despite all the clouds and gloom within you, the Divine still shines its light on you. The light of love, the light of beauty, and the light of inspiration. They are all part of the Divine.

Just like you are.

Shine on, sweet ones.

Muriel

***

August 10, 2014

Interesting! I've asked my guardian angels as to why Michael seems to be showing a lot of interest in me.

Michael heard me and said, "We always protect our messengers more, for we love them deeply. They are ours to care and cherish; they are ours to work with."

Michael has just butted in with a further message:

> Dear one, never worry about your troubles and what is happening now within you, for I'm around and watching. You are one of my messengers, and I will not let any harm come to you. You are precious to us all.
>
> Blessed one, I say that because you are blessed by the Divine and us. You were given to us by the Divine for our purpose in your lifetime. You are our source of laughter, joy, and even love. And we return that to you threefold. You are one that is treasured.
>
> Zaphriel is your protector and will protect your back.
>
> We all love you and will protect strongly what we love. You are never alone, and we won't let you go.
>
> Go with love, and we will surround you with ours. Let this be of comfort, and I don't mind if others

see this. For it shows we share this everlasting and infinite love with all.

I see the tears of joy. This is a way I can communicate with you, as I feel you are equally comfortable with it. And it helps that when you have a clear mind when this happens.

Be at peace; you are with us always. Besides, we have plans for you, and woe betide anyone who mucks around with those and you. I've got your back also.

See ya, kid!

Michael

***

August 11, 2014

Daily Message from the Angels

There is a song in your heart that comes from your spirit. You can feel its gentle joy when you are at peace. During those moments, let that song come through and run through your body.

The pleasure and beauty of the song are such that you will experience such ecstasy and love.

Sing your songs, my little birds.

Raguel

***

August 11, 2014

Due to me forgetting to bring my easel to do a psychic art session and being short-sighted at the same time, this drawing was done at an angle, so it kind of looks a bit distorted. My apologies! I know who the drawing is about; it's Uriel.

***

August 12, 2014

Feeling groggy, with a headache banging on my skull. I tried to do some readings, which didn't help. Now my head is aching away. I've just been told by my guide to relax and stop.

Muriel then told me that I'm still changing, and the other angels are stepping back to give me space to help me cope. My guardian angels and my guides are a rock to me at this moment.

Fifteen minutes later …

Just a few minutes ago, Gabriel turned up beside me and placed his hand on my arm. With a smile, he said, "Please come with me. I am to take you somewhere." He put me in a near instant trance state.

Soon we were both soaring upwards through a tunnel, which I use to visualise going to the higher levels. Gabriel was a bit in front of me, repeating, "Keep up, follow me!"

Finally, we reached a place where it seemed that everything was softly glowing white. It was like an arena of light, and there appeared to be some other angels around. Gabriel gently led me to one that was standing apart from the others. Gabriel turned to me. "This is my world, and at this moment it is yours." Gabriel then introduced me to the one standing separate: Archangel Jeremiel.

Jeremiel reached up and touched my face; he gently touched the part of my head that was aching. As he did this, his hand went inside my head, and he said, "I'm removing a block."

After that, I felt a surge of energy, making my physical body spasm in my chair.

Jeremiel quietly commented, "I'm opening a door for you now." He picked up a glowing crystalline object in his hand and held it near my forehead. A pink light that had specks of deep red in it appeared from the crystal, and the crystal began to glow white. A ray of light shot from the crystal, hit my forehead, and went into my head. I began to spasm again in my chair. Jeremiel asked for someone to hold me still, and the spasms stopped.

He brought the crystal closer and closer, and then he pushed it into my forehead. He turned to Gabriel, saying, "Now take her back."

I turned around and looked at what I was seeing. I saw landscapes of beauty. There was a white tower in the distance. I saw Gabriel standing behind me, and Jeremiel was to my other side. By this time, I started to spasm again.

Gabriel reached forward and gently held me close. "It'll be a quicker journey back if I take you." Gabriel brought me back to my body within a few seconds. I merged back with my body, and I was still slightly spasming.

Now, my headache has been replaced by a feeling of pressure on that side. This is my sign that I'm now downloading again. My vision has gone a bit strange, as if I see things normally, yet I'm seeing a bit outside of normal, if that makes any sense!

I've just been told that I've now gone up a level and that an extradimensional crystal has been put into my third eye.

***

August 12, 2014

Daily Message from the Angels

Darling ones, have you loved yourself today? Given yourself a compliment? If not, do so now! Tell yourself how much you are happy that you are you. Tell yourself that you are looking good. Tell yourself that you enjoy being you. Yes, even tell yourself that you find yourself to be a fun person.

This works best if you stand in front of a mirror. Then you can freely tell yourself all that I have mentioned and more. This is a real confidence booster for you all. And it is true also. You are all such marvellous people.

Be well, my treasures.

Gabriel

***

August 13, 2014

Daily Message from the Angels

Dear ones, when night comes into your house, let it wrap around you in its arms of comfort. Let it rest you for the night. For it is the night that heals your soul, your heart, and your mind. This healing is what you call sleep. It is essential that you rest and heal yourselves during this. For your sleeping moments are the times we angels come to you, talk to your soul, and to give advice. That is the time you and us will commune. It is time the barriers are lifted between us.

If you still cannot rest, then meditation is the next best thing. For it has the same healing abilities as sleep, and it weakens the barriers also.

I know that amongst you, there are those who cannot sleep or rest at all. We understand, and we will wait until you call upon us to help you rest.

Be well.

Raphael

***

August 13, 2014

Another pencil sketch of mine. This one I had a bit more time with. The model kept looking over my shoulder and telling me to do corrections: remove the line, erase shading, more shading …! Geez! I thought Metatron was the only critic of my art. This one was getting into the act as well.

Stop laughing, Raphael. Stop laughing. Yes, you guessed it! This is Raphael.

***

August 14, 2014

Daily Message from the Angels

Do not let the light within you become smothered by the darkness of others. If those people are trying to pull you down from the light into their darkness, walk away. If you cannot leave, shield yourself.

Call upon me if you find yourself fighting the darkness. For when you fight it, it means that the darkness has a hold on you. Call me; I will help.

The best course of action is to avoid getting involved with the darkness in the first place. How? Walk away.

Be well.

Michael

***

August 14, 2014

What happens when you do a pencil sketch of an angel with a sense of humour? Chaos! This one wouldn't stop making faces at me. This is my healing angel Meriel.

***

August 14, 2014

A couple of days ago, I went up a step. Normally I know within a day or two what strengths or new skills I have obtained.

This morning, I got the impression my healing angel was concerned that I didn't seem to show any sign of any changes. He had a quick look at my third eye and found nothing amiss. He told me to wait because he'd be back soon, and he vanished.

Soon he came back with Raphael. Raphael had a quick check; nothing amiss there either. Raphael concluded that I simply didn't know my next step. He told me to close my eyes and tune in.

Well, it appears that my ability for remote viewing has gone up a few notches, and my ability for prophecy has shot up. I've always been strong in those areas, but I've always had to go into a heavy trance to do it. Now I don't have to trance. Yahoo!

Also, my ability to see the angels has gone up a notch. Right now, I "see" the odd glowing light that indicates one of my guides is around. The angels have a bigger light—much bigger! They take human form if they feel like a chat with me. My guides are presences that are felt around me at this moment. I can certainly see them better when they want my attention. My guardian angels are also presences felt around me too.

Meriel is to the left of me, peering over my shoulder, elbow on the back of my chair, and grinning like the Cheshire cat because he's reading this.

I think I'm going to be busy fine-tuning this lot.

***

August 15, 2014

Daily Message from the Angels

Things are looking up for you all. There is a shift in the world that is starting to be felt by all. A shift in the vibrations to the light.

Ever felt moved by an emotion that is so close to love and so strong? It is the first sign. Relax, hold on to that feeling, relish the love coming down, and watch the shift's effects on your world spreading. It is done for all of you. Be part of the moment and be part of this shift. Spread this love and your light around.

Above all, believe in the true light that is within your soul, for it is the light that was placed there by the Divine.

Be well, beautiful ones, for I watch you all with love.

Gabriel

***

August 15, 2014

A message from Chamuel.

I am Chamuel, and I have my message to give to everyone.

All of you want to grow and develop beyond your current level in your abilities. That is a wonderful and worthy cause to aim for. For it is the lightworkers' creed to grow, enlarge, and spread out the light of Divine love and the Divine word.

Let me help you with this. For love is my speciality, and I channel the Divine's love to you all. Ask me to come to you and implant this seed of Divine love. Call upon me.

I will now tell you how to help it grow. As the seed of this love is planted, surround it with your own love. Let this love be unconditional and have no boundaries. For that is what our love for you is like.

Feed that love to this seed within and protect it. In doing so, this seed will grow inside of you, nurtured by your very presence. This seed of love will then grow into the very essence of Divine love and will embed its loving roots around you, embracing you, to the very core of you. We are infusing you with greater love. And it is this that the Divine will then touch you with its light upon you.

The young, planted love will then open into the most beautiful blossom of all: you! You will be the purest flower giving out your love to all, and you will shine with this love, for its cause will be Divine love. And the fruits of this love will spread. It will bring you to greater heights in your life. It will be pure, and it will be you.

I do so love you all, and I want this to be for you: to grow and become one with the Divine in the loving light. We all want this to happen, for when it has spread far enough, your vibration and the vibration of your world will heighten to new levels. And the next level is beautiful. I want you to see it and eagerly await your presence.

If there are those who still deny this and refuse to absorb the Divine's love, then I am afraid you may be left behind in the cold. This is not good, and the thought of it saddens me greatly. Please, don't back away but come forward and accept it.

I ask my lightworkers to help in bringing in those who hide away from the light. Show them that there is nothing to fear, but there's plenty to love.

Please, I do ask of this, and I know that some of you have very busy lives. But it is easier than you think. All you must do is show that another person love.

So little, so much, and so effective.

I thank you all with my love, Divine love, and universal love.

Bless you, all my lightworkers. For I also love you all.

Chamuel

***

August 15, 2014

There is a feeling of a cold breeze wafting around me. There is no breeze in my room. The cause is that of Gabriel, who is playing games with me: Touching my neck, then my shoulder, then a hand, and even the side of my face.

I tuned in.

He wanted me to play a guessing game as to who was touching me. A bit of teasing was given to me, and then he started singing a little ditty.

Yep! Gabriel! The only one who is mischievous enough to do this, and one of the biggest pranksters of the lot. He's fun, clever, loving, and very wise, and he makes me laugh all the time.

I love these guys!

***

August 16, 2014

Daily Message from the Angels

Welcome the beginning of a new day. It is the start of a new idea, a new promise, and a new future. Let the sense of adventure unfold as does the day unfold for you too.

Each new day is another step towards us. Each breath is a step towards the light. Each ounce of love is a step towards more love.

Walk forward, revel in your day, and say to yourself, "I am! I will! I can!" Then feel the words changing you from within. For these words are powerful tools of confirmation and positive change. That change is called confidence, joy, and self-belief. All are treasured by us because they are of the higher vibrations.

This is what your new day brings to you. Go and tell the world how wonderful your day is going to be. We and the world will hear you. In turn, you will start to make other people's day into a day of joy.

Be well.

Michael

***

August 17, 2014

Daily Message from the Angels

Let us talk about freedom.

Some of you have your own ideas, I am sure. But I have my own.

Freedom to love.
Freedom to sing.
Freedom to dance with joy.
Freedom to take a chance.
Freedom to make your own decision in life.
Freedom to select your own mate.

So many more I can name. But to me, these are important.

Please accept these freedoms as your own given right. Let no one take them away from you. These are the freedoms the Divine has given you to use. No one can change that fact. And it was all for you and you alone. If anyone tries to force their restrictions on you, take advantage of another freedom that is yours: the freedom to be free.

Enjoy it; these are wonderful freedoms to have. Use them, love them, and above all enjoy them.

I leave you now with my message

Be well, my dearest ones. Be well.

Raguel

***

August 17, 2014

This was a message Gabriel channelled through me earlier today.

There is nothing so important in this world than you. You are important to family, to friends, and to us. You are wonderful, beautiful and perfect. Yes! You are!

Perfection is in the eyes of God. God made you, so you were made perfect because God made you.

Your life in the past has had many pitfalls, but there have been many great events. Learn from the past. Once learned, let the memories go where you want them to go.

Your life in the present is equally varied. Learn from this and let it go into the past.

As to your life in the future, you will learn again, and the result is you will come nearer to God.

Learn and grow towards the blessed light of love; you will become closer to God. This is wonderful for us. Growth, learning, and love are all the aims of your soul. Once all the aspects of these are learned, you will go towards the next level, towards God.

Be blessed and grow with love!

Gabriel

***

August 18, 2014

Daily Message from the Angels

Let us into your heart, and we will fill it with our love.
Let us into your life, and we will fill it with happiness.
Let us into your soul, and we will fill it with the light.
We are Love, we are of happiness, and we are of the light.
You are Love, you are the happiness, and you are of the light.

Remember that every day of your life, believe in it, and believe in us just like we believe in you. You are each a part of the Divine, just like we are.

We welcome you to the Divine's love.

Be love.

Azrael

***

August 19, 2014

Daily Message from the Angels

Let the music of the birds sing to your soul. They call praises of their world to us. They sing of the joy of the day. They tell us of the Divine's glory that is covering their world, and they love it.

Be like the birds, my sweet ones. Sing to our souls. Call the praises of your world to us. Sing your song of joy for today. Tell us how blessed you feel when the Divine's glory touches you with love. We are always listening to you.

Sing the song that is within your soul, because it produces the music so beautiful.

Be blessed.

Ariel

***

August 20, 2014

Daily Message from the Angels

Relax; do not worry about small things. Do not worry about large things. You are not in control over them, so why let them get to you? Many people have problems, big and little. Don't worry about these, as no problem is big enough to warrant the stress.

Instead, relax and think this: You are not in control of other's problems. You never were in control. They are not yours to control in the first place. Just relax and let things go. Just enjoy your life to the fullest. For it is your life, after all. Only you can control that.

Be well.

Jophiel

***

August 21, 2014

Did a bit of artwork this morning while watching TV. Gabriel wanted me to draw his portrait and wouldn't let me watch TV in peace, so out came the art gear.

Gabriel kept showing me pictures of what face poses he was going to do, just to stir it up with me, but he resorted to the classic portrait. That didn't stop him teasing me, but he did insist on his hair being this way. I took my time on this picture.

I got the impression that he had a glyph on his forehead, but I couldn't make it out. I also felt he was hiding it.

His reason: that I didn't know it yet, and it was a bit complicated.

So here is his portrait.

Not very good. Not one of my better pictures.

***

August 21, 2014

Daily Message from the Angels

There is a big world out there that's full of adventures, experiences, and wonders. That world is for you to play in. Play within its grounds and waters. Enjoy the feel of nature and the touch of the sun caressing your cheek. Dance in the rain; it is cleansing and is nature's way of saying, "I love you." Dance in the rain, embrace the light of the sun, sing to the moon, and give your soul a chance to enjoy nature.

Be part of all this wondrous world of miracles. For you were all put here for one specific purpose: to learn and enjoy your learning experiences.

Be well, my beloved ones.

Gabriel

***

August 21, 2014

By special request from Angel Rachel: a picture of Chamuel.

Sam (Chamuel's nickname, as his name is pronounced Samuel) was very eager to have a portrait done. Didn't even clown about or dither. Just got ready and focused on me.

My reward for the picture? Chamuel gave me a hug.

Again, not one of my better pictures.

***

August 22, 2014

Daily Message from the Angels

Beloved ones, do not let others take your power away. For it is your power and yours alone. Instead, keep your power close to you and walk away from those who would try to control you.

You are a spiritual being of such beauty and strength that those who are weaker than you will try to take what is yours. So be strong, rise above them and above all, and send them on their way with love. Never look back. Go forward, be yourself, and show your inner light to the world. You are strong and powerful in your very own right.

Be blessed, my children. For though you are many, you are also one.

Anael

***

August 23, 2014

Daily Message from the Angels

Let love be your guide, for it will never lose your path. Love is within you all, as it was placed there by the Divine. Love is your path; love is your messenger. It is a path to peace, light, and universal wonders.

The Divine is love. The universe is made with love; you are made of love. You are love personified. You are, after all, part of the Divine also.

Spread the love, my beautiful ones. Spread the love.

Ariel

***

August 24, 2014

Daily Message from the Angels

When things go wrong, do not despair. You are not alone in your pain. We are around, healing, loving, and caring.

We are the ones who will never leave you. We are the ones who will always love you. We are the ones who will always be at your side. We are the ones who will comfort you.

Who are we? We are your angels, your friends, your spiritual family. We will never ever leave you alone, for we are always around you. Let us into your life and accept us in your hearts. For we love you far more than you realise.

Be well my beloved ones,

Raphael

***

August 25, 2014

Daily Message from the Angels

Beloved ones, are you not aware of the world around you? Are you not caring for her? Whom am I talking about? I am talking about your world—Gaia is her name. She is your mother, and you are all sorely neglecting her. She wants you to come home to her and share her life with you so that you can be of Gaia again.

You have all been apart for too long, and now Gaia wants her children to come home. Gaia is loving and nurturing. Gaia is within you, but you hide from her. Come home to your mother, my blessed ones. Come home to her and love her, for she loves you. Care for her, for she cares for you. Be kind to her, and she is kind to you.

But she does miss her beloved children. And it pains her to see her children fighting amongst themselves. No more, please, and be at peace with each other. Fighting solves no problems. Come home!

I thank you for hearing me.

Ambriel

***

August 26, 2014

Daily Message from the Angels

Beloved ones, let the light of the sky shine on you. Let the sun embrace you with its warmth. They are there to show that there are no barriers to you, but the ones you make yourselves. The sky has no limits; the sun is not tied to one spot but orbits in the universe.

You are not tied to one spot either. You are a free person who can go anywhere you want. You can make yourself into anything you want.

The gifts that enable you to do this is within you. Your own spirit is infinite. Your own heart always has room for more love. You are your own master. So soar into your life like the eagle soars in the sky, free and open to the world.

Fly, my birds, fly.

Ambriel

***

August 26, 2014

Last night, Archangel Ambriel wanted me to draw his portrait. I told him to wait until the morning. When morning came, I got my pencils and pad and got drawing.

Ambriel showed me his face twice to see that I got it right, and he even stood over my shoulder and told me when to stop drawing.

Right now, he's just told me he is pleased with it.

***

August 27, 2014

Daily Message from the Angels

Welcome to my world. The sky is bright with the sun. The grass is green with life. The waters are abundant with the force of nature. The animals and people walk upon my world within the light of day.

Love the light.

There are the animals who walk upon the world under the stars and the moon. They too walk under the light of another kind.

Love the light.

The moonlight, sunlight, and starlight are one. The creator made them all with love, made them all for you to love, and made you all out of their love.

The reason why?

You love the creations made by the Divine; treasure its beauty. You are one of the many creations; love thy self for what you are: created with the light of love. You are wonderful, you are beautiful, and you are perfect. You are part of the creator, and the creator is the Divine, so you all have part of the Divine within you.

To the Creator, you are perfect. To me, you are perfect. To the universe, you are perfect. So why hide your perfectness behind false illusions and lies? This makes no sense to me.

Think of my words, beautiful ones.

Be well.

Jeremiah

Jeremiah was known in biblical times as the weeping prophet.

***

August 28, 2014

Daily Message from the Angels

Just be yourself, for there is no other person as wonderful as you. You are unique in your own special way. Accept that, and you will realise that you are in fact perfect. You see, you are unique and special, and that makes you perfect.

Now, have you looked at yourself in the mirror and stared into your own eyes? There lie your depths of yourself. Your soul, your thoughts, your own inner divinity. Yet again, you are perfect.

Be well, my lovely ones. Be well.

Zadkiel

***

August 29, 2014

Daily Message from the Angels

Will let yourself go to the most beautiful thing in your world? I hear you think, "What is it? What is this beautiful thing you mention?" This thing I mention is your very own inner self, your soul. Have you let yourself touch your very own soul?

There are those who have done so and found something so beautiful that it surpasses any boundaries in your world. That beauty is called love. Touch the love within your own soul, and you will touch the love of God.

Be well, my beloved ones.

Ramiel (Jeremiel)

***

August 30, 2014

Daily Message from the Angels

There is a song in the universe that brings true light to those who hear it. The song of life is the most powerful thing in existence.

The song is of love.
The song is Divine.

When you hear this song go through you, it is the most inspiring source of joy that you will feel. It will bring joy, happiness, and riches of the spirit. The song is of love; let it flow within you. For it is sung by the Divine and us.

Be well.

Raphael

***

August 30, 2014

A Message from Gabriel

I see you all walking in your world; some without a care in their hearts. You're just rushing heedlessly into the next adventure and not caring if your actions destroy others. This is not how it is meant to be. You are meant to care for each other. Love your fellow man, and above all love your world. You are the keepers of your world, and if you intend to ignore that duty, you will find that the world will in turn start to ignore you.

Not a pleasant feeling, I assure you.

Stop for a few minutes before you head off to your next appointment. Look around your world. Did you see a small bird pulling at a blade of grass to make a nest? That is what your world contains. Did you see a child running from one end of a playground to another in a game of tag? That is also in your world. Did you gently touch the petals of a flower nearby, feeling the gentle, soft velvet that it is made of? Your world again.

Such beauties should not be ignored, for they are all part of your world, just like you are. Stop ignoring it and start exploring that part of the world. You will never be disappointed by what you will discover.

Life is nearly infinite in its many varieties. So much to learn, explore, and look at in awe. Yes, your world is beautiful, and it's about time you knew it. Each little flower and bird has a purpose in this world of yours. Each is part of each other and you! Be part of your world, because it is a part of you. You belong here, and so does every living thing on it, from the lowliest microbe to the majestic beauty of a blue whale. They are what makes your world such an interesting and exciting place to visit.

Cherish these moments around you, for they are all unique and will never be repeated. Each little movement and thought are different for every single second in your world. And these moments are infinite, just like you. Believe in these moments; relish them for their spontaneous beauty and everlasting energy. You are part of these moments too and will forever be so.

You are part of this world indeed, right down to the atomic level.

In the words of your people, take the time to smell the roses.

Be blessed, my children, for you are many and yet so few.

Gabriel

***

August 30, 2014

Another picture I did this morning also. Guess who decided to pose? Michael. He gave me a lot of teasing after this.

***

August 31, 2014

As I was working on my PC, I saw a typical angel picture, feathered wings and all. At that moment, Raphael decided to chat. He must have been bored, I think.

I mentioned that feathers would be a big nuisance to look after, and inconvenient at times. He agreed avidly and mentioned that angels are energy beings. He went on to say that angels don't even eat. Being energy meant that they could go places at nearly the speed of thought, can be anywhere they want, and can even go into small spaces. No wings to bother them. They can also move fast and take on any form, and—at this point, I could sense a lighter change in Raphael's voice tone—best of all, they didn't even fart.

At this point, I burst out laughing. I could hear Raphael chuckling away in the background. I love it when he lets his serious side drop, because he has a rather earthy sense of humour.

Thank you, Raphael, I needed that laugh.

***

August 31, 2014

Daily Message from the Angels

Go forward into your future life. Don't stop—don't even look back. What has happened is in the past and cannot be brought back again. This is good, for it means you can let go of what pain you received from past events. You can even let go of people who have made you unhappy. You can also let go of those who have made you happy in the past, and their memories live on within you in a loving light, knowing within yourself that these people and friends are now in a better place, healthy and cured of ills.

Walk forward to your new life, meet new people and new adventures, and see many wonderful new experiences.

Welcome to your world, and welcome to your future.

Be well, my beloved ones, be well.

Raphael

***

August 31, 2014

Here is a picture of my higher self, Emrayel. Here is the story that goes with it.

This morning, I was told by Raphael to test my limits in my abilities. I decided to test the boundaries of my ability to go through the levels ahead of me, and I went into a meditative state. I visualised myself going through a long tunnel. Raphael kept an eye on the proceedings throughout and gave advice in certain parts. Raphael told me to keep on going through this tunnel, and I went a bit further than I usually do, which showed my boundaries had expanded.

As I was nearing this border, I heard Raphael say that Michael would meet me soon to stop me. Sure enough, Michael came through and placed himself in front of me. Michael told me the reason why he stopped me from overstepping my boundaries was to make sure that I never got lost, and that it was the same with all my boundaries. He also mentioned that I was welcome and expected to test them a lot, for how else would I know when I could go further?

Michael rested an arm on my shoulder, quickly conversed with Raphael through my psychic link, and put his face close to mine. (Michael is one very tall being, hitting over twelve feet.) Michael asked me to look into his eyes. I did what he asked me to do, and I found myself in a room that was very beautiful. It had ornate yet simple tastes to it. Very modern with a hint of Turkish bazaar in decorations. It even had a meditation couch that was draped in red silk and had a soft cover with plenty of cushions. It was luxurious and comfortable. Michael told me that this is the place where my higher self resided.

I looked out the window and saw a beautiful view of fields, peaceful blue sky, and clean air.

Michael attracted my attention and put his arm around my shoulder. He mentioned to me that he was going to take me to another room attached and reached forward to open a door. As I entered through this door, I noticed there was a conservatory in the next room, beautiful palm trees, and brightly coloured flowers. In the middle was a seat that had cushions on it.

Sitting in the middle of the seat was this lovely being eyeing me up with amusement. Michael told me this was my higher self, Emrayel, and that they both wanted me to visit.

Emrayel was lovely to look at. Black wavy hair, almond eyes, and golden skin. Emrayel wore a dark red robe and had a dark amethyst or onyx neckband. Emrayel was glowing with a lilac aura. It had a golden jewel in the middle of the forehead that glowed gold light.

They both spoke to me about how it was high time for me to meet my higher self. If I was having difficulties with any of my abilities, I could call upon Emrayel to help. Then Emrayel told me that the time would come when we would both merge minds into one. I would become Emrayel because I am an aspect of Emrayel's will and personality. Emrayel also mentioned that I was given the aspect of intelligence, psychic ability, and art. I also had strong will and wisdom installed in me.

Soon Michael added that it was time for me to meet some more people, and we all said, "See you later," or something similar.

Michael put his arm around my shoulder again and carried me through to another world. I found myself hurtling into a world that was green with trees and had a floating city in the sky ahead of me. But instead of going to the city, I found myself heading towards a white-glowing, ground-based city in the middle of the jungle. We landed outside the city.

There waiting for us was this man with Middle Eastern features. He indicated that I should walk with him. We walked to a glade that looked familiar to me. The man pointed out a log for me to sit on. He introduced himself as Khalid and said that this glade was the same spot where I was first introduced to my spirit guides. He stated that I had reached the stage where I was to be introduced to some of the ascended masters. He added that one other would be here very soon.

Within a few seconds, a bright light appeared to one side. This light contained a youthful yet wise face with straight blonde hair, blue eyes, and a gentle expression to his face. This being sat on the log beside me and mentioned that we were to work together often. That was why I was brought here, to meet with the two ascended masters with whom I would be dealing.

He introduced Khalid as Serapis Bey. The name Khalid was either a nickname, or he didn't want to overwhelm me at the beginning. The blonde master beside me introduced himself as Ashtar, and he showed me the stars around us.

Ashtar spoke. "That there are billions upon billions of worlds out there, and each has its own Gaia to nurture them. All the lives on these worlds are the children of their own Gaias. All are connected by one thing: the power of the Divine."

He mentioned that I had touched the mind of the Divine, but I had been held back to make sure that I wasn't absorbed into it, because the human mind cannot cope with the immensity, power, and depth of the Divine's mind. I would have ceased to be. This barrier stopping me had been placed there by the Divine itself. And it was the Divine's wish that it was time to meet the ascended masters.

Soon Ashtar brought me back to where I was, in the glade and sitting on a log, and told me that it was time for me to go back home.

The masters and Michael spoke for a short while, and then Michael held me close and said he'd get me back quickly. Within seconds, I found myself zooming to my own world and straight to my house.

Michael stayed for a short while to make sure all was well and said that it was now my time to explore my abilities. He also said that Raphael had created the link with me because it appeared that I was "going places". He bent forward, kissed my forehead, and left.

I woke up, and Raphael was beside and was amused by the whole thing. He mentioned that I could draw Emrayel if I wanted to, because Emrayel would be happy to let me. Also, if I needed any help with parts of Emrayel's face, I could call upon Emrayel to show themselves (yes, Emrayel is neither male nor female).

I drew the picture.

***

August 31, 2014

A message came through me later today at the church.

> Will you let us welcome you to my world of the light and love? Will you let us enjoy the laughter and the love you send us? Yes! You will indeed, for we do welcome you to our world of music, light, and love.
>
> Will you welcome us to your world? In your homes and in your hearts? Again, you will. For when we come into your lives, we bring our world of miracles into yours.
>
> Let us join with you in adoring the Divine One! The Divine One is our creator—yours and mine. Love is our common bond, for in that we are one united. This is wonderful for all of us. Let us celebrate our lives, our loves and our ultimate parent, the Divine One. Let that love of the Divine One rest in our inner selves, for it transcends all barriers and raises our own selves in the eyes of the Divine One.
>
> Please welcome that Divine love into your hearts. Welcome it in your souls, for it is eternal and infinite, and so is your soul.
>
> Be well in the Divine light and be filled with the Divine's love.

You are all beautiful and perfect. Show yourself to the world that you are this Divine perfection.

Be blessed, for you are all mine to love.

Gabriel

***

September 1, 2014

Daily Message from the Angels

Beloved ones, let peace rule you and let it live with you, for it is much better than fighting. Mediate and share information; don't fight over it.

You are all the same underneath. You have the same world to live on—the same emotions and the same lives. Please let peace have a chance to live within you. It is not hard to do this. Just stop all conflict and let us start the love within you.

Are you willing to do this for us? If so, tell us out loud with your voice and your hearts. Tell us. We are listening to everything you say.

Bless you all.

Serapis Bey

***

September 2, 2014

Daily Message from the Angels

When you join your love with that of the Divine's, you are joining two powerful forces into one. This force can change worlds. It can change destinies. It can change you, for your love is strong, and when merged with the Divine's own life force, which is love also, then miracles can happen.

Don't hide your love but join it with ours in loving the Divine. Spread that love for all to feel. Now watch the miracles appear.

Barachiel

***

September 3, 2014

Daily Message from the Angels

Have you ever sat down and done something just for yourself, because you enjoy doing it? A hobby that gives you great pleasure is your moment to rest and recharge. Take time out for yourself at regular intervals and often. For as you rest and recharge, you are also learning to advance. These moments of rest are our moments to heal you and teach you.

We feel your enjoyment as you work on your hobbies; we watch with great interest. It is a wonderful thing that you do, and often enough, a hobby often brings out the skilled crafts master within you.

Enjoy your personal free times. Enjoy those moments of rest. Never be ashamed to have your alone times, for in those times you are sorting out your innermost thoughts and calming down. Never let anyone take these moments away from you because you need them for your health and spiritual well-being.

Be blessed, my friends.

Ariel

***

September 4, 2014

Daily Message from the Angels

Beloved ones, do you believe in the Divine? Well, you should. After all, the Divine believes in you, and the Divine lives within every single one of you. The Divine knows you better than you know yourself, for you are one of the Divine's many creations. You will never be forsaken or forgotten by the Divine because of this connection. You will forever remain in the Divine's love and sight.

Take comfort that the Divine has only love for you, not vengeance. For the Divine is love. The Divine cannot feel hate.

Be well and think about this.

Believe!

Mary Magdalene

***

September 5, 2014

Daily Message from the Angels

Go forward amidst confusion and disarray, for if you stay, you will become part of the disorder. I say again, go forward and leave behind the chaos. As you step forward, you will step into love. You will step into the light, and you will step into a new future.

Leave behind the part of your past that no longer serves you. You are free from any pain the past has given you. It is in the past and finished with. It cannot return to harm you anymore.

Let go! Let God! Let love!

Be free and head towards the light of a new world.

Muriel

***

September 6, 2014

Daily Message from the Angels

Those who do not love you, let them go. Those who do not care for you, let them go. Those that feed on your energy, let them go.

You don't need them.

Look for someone who will love you, care for you, and give support back. They are the ones we have chosen for you. They are everywhere, so don't blind yourself to them.

Be well.

Haniel

***

September 7, 2014

Daily Message from the Angels

As you lie down at night and prepare to rest, call upon us to keep your family safe. For each member, there is an infinite multitude of us watching over you. We will keep your family and friends safe. We do this because we love you.

Call upon us. We will hear from you. Don't be shy about this; we can see through you to your heart. You ask us to keep your family safe because you love them. We love you in return for asking us, and we also love your family. Call upon us. We will hear you and answer you with love.

Be blessed.

Geliel

***

September 7, 2014

A Message from AA Azrael

You are what the world needs. You are its saviour. Stand up and reclaim the love, the colour and the variety that nature has given you.

Stop those who wish to remove that beautiful part of Gaia, the part called nature.

Each living thing in your world was placed here to teach you, to entertain you, and to feed you. Don't let those who wish to destroy nature with their bulldozers and cranes. That is not the way it is meant to be.

You are created side by side with each creature. You were meant to look after each other in harmony and compassion. That is what nature was made for. Instead, nature is pulled apart by machines. This is not the way it is meant to be.

To fix it, give nature your love. Look after your part of the world, for the world is too big to be watched over by only a few. Each of you should look after your own small part. Your race is all over the world, so each small part looked after can span nearly all the world. Believe in that. We do.

I have also noticed that those who commit crimes against others have created a disturbance. This is not the way it is meant to be.

You were made to love one another, not fight. For in numbers combined and united, you are the strongest source of strength and love the universe has ever seen. Look at your neighbour and friends, unite in comradeship and love, and push away those negative energies that will try to take over.

Don't give the negativity a chance, and you will grow strong. United, you stand; divided, you will fall. Be one with each other and develop your power. You are all stronger together but are weak apart. Your destiny in the stars shows that your kind will expand outwards to new worlds, but only if you are all united. Let this be true, for when you have walked in the light and have absorbed the light, you will be welcome to what is beyond your world. And it is beautiful.

Be in mind of what I have said, for I wish for all to be one in unification and in love.

Be well, my children, be well.

Azrael

***

September 8, 2014

Daily Message from the Angels

Let those who can fly to the sky in their imagination do so, for they have the sight to see beyond the walls that surround them. These are the dreamers who can create wonders around them, for they are your inventors, artists, and entertainers. Be like them and see beyond your circle, beyond your walls.

Dream.

As you dream, you create. As you create, you manifest. As you manifest, you grow your own future.

Dream, and make your dreams become a reality. You have that power and always will. Just believe in yourself.

Gabriel

***

September 9, 2014

Daily Message from the Angels

Trust in yourself. Trust in your spirit and trust in your guardian angels, for they are pure and are only for you. You know yourself better than anyone.

Your spirit is the one who will warn you of conflict and danger. And your guardian angels will always guide, protect, and love you. Their bond between you and them is unbreakable. That bond is for you alone.

When the love for each other becomes mutual, you will begin that wonderful path of enlightenment. They will lead you, save you from stumbling, and give you the courage to go on. That is a path to a great new you and a wonderful future.

Love each other.

Michael

***

September 10, 2014

Daily Message from the Angels

Walk the path of peace and love, for that is the path towards perfection—perfection in your spirit and perfection in the eyes of the Divine. You have that ability; you have that choice. Walk that path to your ultimate destiny: love embodied. Love is perfection.

As you step forward, you are accepting the Divine One into your homes and hearts, and therefore the start of your growth to the light.

Children, you are in the eyes of the Divine to be cared for, loved, and nurtured. As you grow up, you become stronger, are open to more adventures in spirit, and will develop into the ultimate you: ascendancy.

Your soul is perfect as it is, but it needs to learn more to become more of the light. That is why it chose you and incarnated as you: to learn, and to help you learn. Learn and love.

Be with love, my lovely ones,

Haniel

***

September 11, 2014

Daily Message from the Angels

Let your love light shine forth, bringing those who are of similar mind to your presence. When they do arrive at your door, shine that light of yours brighter and envelope these people. For they are of the same light as you and wish to share theirs with yours.

In joining of such light, you will grow stronger in vibrations and spiritual development.

This light will bring you all forward, and in doing so, you will be spreading the word of the light, the word of the One, and the word of universal peace.

Shine on, my diamond children,

Michael

***

September 12, 2014

Daily Message from the Angels

This is a time of memories and self-retrospection. Send your love to those who have moved on from this world to the next. Send your blessings to those who have gone before you.

They are your past, your present, and now your future. Be strong in what they have given you in life, for it is the same in their world now.

You won't fail them by letting them go forward. Instead, you are rewarding them. You are in a way telling them that they are free to grow, to come back to visit you. That is what they did in your world. Well, it's happening in ours.

Never let go of the memory, but instead, let go of the pain. Take time to remember and cherish that memory.

Be at peace, my children, be at peace.

Malach

***

September 13, 2014

Daily Message from the Angels

Let those who serve you well become your greatest friends. Let those who love you unconditionally become your new family. Let those who offer a helping hand when no one else does become your allies in life. These are the most precious examples of what we want in your life. These simple acts are called love.

Welcome these people to your world and become part of theirs at the same time.

Let the beauty of it spread.

Ambrose

***

September 14, 2014

Daily Message from the Angels

Beloved ones, do you know what is exactly going on in your world? Do you see the sunrise in the morning and relish the beauty it contains? Do you enjoy the sound of the birds singing in their claims of joy? Do you even know of the hard-working bee collecting from one flower to another?

You seem to be too engrossed in the bad news around your world. This is not good because it gives that negativity power. Instead, enjoy the good things in life; enjoy nature and its many wonders. You will find that such negativity will lose its power when it finds that no one is feeding it. Think about that, my friends. Think about that.

Be well.

Michael

***

September 15, 2014

Daily Message from the Angels

Beloved ones, do you not love one another? If so, show it! Say it! Live it! These are all things that you can do for each other. A simple touch of the hand or even a smile can be the simplest and easiest way to express that. Such small gestures can lead to much bigger love in your hearts. So please, accept what comes your way, and give back the same in return. A little goes a long way, and a long way goes deep.

What are you all waiting for? Spread the love.

Gabriel

***

September 16, 2014

Daily Message from the Angels

Keep it simple. If it is complicated, then it isn't meant to be.
The best things in life are easily seen, heard, felt, and around.
If you must fight or struggle for it, then it is not meant for you.
Keep it free, and in turn you will be free.
Keep it simple, and in turn you will find your problems leave you.
Keep it alive, and in turn you will live a fuller life.

And above all keep it within the light, for the light lives within you.

Gabriel

***

September 17, 2014

Daily Message from the Angels

Have you ever decided to have a good wander around in your town? Pick a street at random and walk to the end; maybe pick a direction to walk to next. Just to have a walk with your own thoughts and to explore.

This act of randomness may not be as random as you think, for it could be us directing you to a path that you need to follow. And it is the same with your path in life. You think you are wandering about and at random directions, but it isn't so. No matter how much you move about, you will always end up where you are meant to be. There may be delays, but the result will be the same.

Out of the many paths, the best one will be the easiest, the most enlightening, and the most perfect.

That is how it is meant to be, my dears.

Be well.

Cassiel

***

September 18, 2014

Daily Message from the Angels

Just be aware of what is going on around you, my sweet ones. For even though things may be dragging slowly to you, they are in fact your destiny coming into line.

You may think that your journey from your job to your home is too slow. Think again. Aren't you finding that extra waiting time just right to sort things out in your mind, to contemplate the beauty of nature, and to put things into perspective? Yes, that is the time that is not wasted.

An appointment that takes too long? Accept that and relax. Use the time to daydream. Daydreams are good for you. Enjoy them, because we do.

All is happening and never still, even when you think you are at a standstill. And you are not. Birds fly, bees hover from flower to flower, clouds pass by, and even the world is in constant motion. Your heart beats; your thoughts flit like fireflies in the night. You are surrounded by action, and even your destiny involves these little, hidden things.

You are part of this world of yours, and you can't escape it. In fact, who wants to? It is beautiful, and it is yours. Your destiny is to look after your world. It is all you have.

Be with the light.

Amasras

***

September 19, 2014

Daily Message from the Angels

Laugh like there is no worry in the world. Laugh like you really wanted to laugh like. Don't hold back and relish the moment of laughter. Don't worry about tomorrow; it will come. But if you laugh at the so-called problems that it brings, you will find your inner strength. Those problems aren't really that foreboding, are they? They are smaller than you thought they were. These problems will soon pass. They are problems because you made a simple lesson into a big mass of worry.

Instead, laugh at it. See it for what it is: a lesson. Learn from it and then move on from it. As you laugh, your joy comes up to us and pleases the Divine. It pleases us too.

So, laugh away with the joy of life, nature, The Divine and Love. You will find others will laugh with you. These are kindred souls who share your moment of Light. Relish their company.

Forget the past; it is of no concern to us and you. Your past is of lessons that you have learnt. It is over and done with. Move on.

I await your laughter, my sweet ones, and will join you in it.

Be with the light of love.

Gabriel

***

September 20, 2014

Daily Message from the Angels

When the music of the light reaches your soul, let your soul dance. Let your soul sing to it. And your soul will shine brighter than it has ever shone before. You will be a beacon of light because you have let the Divine light show itself from within you.

This is a small but very necessary step in your journey of learning and love, and it's to one destiny: ascendancy.

Shine on, my sweet stars, and you will shine your love to the Divine.

Glow, shine, and be with us in love.

Chamuel

***

September 20, 2014

The latest update to me, which happened during a midday meditation today. Archangel Chamuel came to visit me, and he told me to go into a meditative state. I did as he asked, and this is what happened.

As I sank deeper into this meditation, Chamuel placed his hands on the top of my head. Soon I found myself moving forward at high speed down a tunnel and towards a bright light. I knew this meant I was going through the dimensions and towards the angelic level.

When I reached there, faces flickered into view and faded back out. One face remained and showed itself as an angel. This angel took me into a room that had brightly lit, white glowing walls. There was nothing in this room but one gold ornamentation, which was in the centre.

As I was brought to this ornamentation, another humanlike form began to take shape. This one had near white gold hair and wore loose white clothing. He approached me and began speaking to me and of me about needing direction. He agreed that I needed more than just to be told to go forward if I'm not told where to move forward to. He said that my power levels had reached the stage in which more boundaries needed to be removed, due to my ability to flit from one dimension to another with my mind. Other things were spoken of, but I can't remember them.

I asked his name, and his reply was, "There is no need for you to know." A voice in my head told me that this was one of the ascended masters. His name started with M, I think; I didn't catch the name so can't relate it.

The angel that came with me was told by this master to take me deeper into the building. We entered another room which, by rights, defied normal physics. As I looked up through a windowed ceiling, I saw a large eye watching me through a massive, glowing sphere of light that was floating outside. The eye became part of a face that showed and was absorbed back into the energy. I got the impression that this was the Divine watching over me and letting me know.

A door in front of me opened, and a bright, blinding light poured from it. I was led inside by the angel. I stood there looking around me and noticed what appeared to be a reclining male human form floating in the middle of this white light, which rotated him into the standing position. This one walked forward towards me and stopped close. He looked at me closely, raised his hand (which was glowing with white light), and placed it on my forehead.

He greeted me and related to me that he was removing boundaries and opening more doors, generally giving me a boost. He also informed me that it was now time that I started fully channelling the masters. This was what I was trained for, and now it was time.

He told me that someone would be sent to give me that direction. He spoke of how my words were now reaching the world and going farther. I was to now develop that skill more. I am to remain to teach others, for that is part of my destiny too. Some will reach my level of skill, some may not, and some may go beyond but in another direction. My path was to make sure they get there. I still have a lot to learn, but due to the boundaries being removed, all that knowledge will be ready for me to use.

He told the angel beside me to take me back. As I looked back at this master, I asked, "Is that you, Ashtar?" His response was to smile and confirm it was.

The angel beside me began to carry me back to my body. It was then that we started talking. I realised the angel was Michael, which was confirmed by the nickname he uses for me, "Little Sister". I sensed another beside me coming up, and I looked around and saw Gabriel. He was laughing and appeared happy. I sensed the third one above me and looked up to see Raziel. He looked pleased.

As I was settled in my body, I was kept in the meditative state by Chamuel. Raziel had moved on, but Michael and Gabriel remained. They both knelt beside me and spoke of a new path coming up for me. They would let me know when I was to take it, adding that my job situation is being worked on.

Michael told me that my guardian angels were to help me in this next stage, so I had to let them take over in parts. He pointed out one guardian angel and said that Darryl was to be my cautious side and would help me avoid getting caught into something that was not meant for me. I must say Darryl did have that thick mop of unruly curly black hair that I drew him with, beard and all.

Michael pointed at another guardian angel and said that Fleur was to help me in my work by making sure that I am energised, kept calm, and focussed. She was to help by giving me stability. And, yes, Fleur is even more beautiful than my picture of her indicated. She's lovely with long blonde hair, a pink-flowered coronal, blue eyes, and a sweet expression.

And finally, Michael pointed to a third guardian angel and said that Zaphriel was to be my protector and will keep negative energies or people away from me. He was also to be my strength and friend. Well, Zaphriel was even better looking than I'd expected. I drew his picture, but the reality was much better. Wavy dark blond hair, dark brown eyes with humour in them, strong and brooding features, and a look of determination.

Michael came close, kissed my third eye, and put his forehead against mine. He stated he loved me and then placed his hands on my face. Then the third eye kisses again, and he backed away.

Gabriel reached forward and did the third eye kiss. He laughed and said he loved me as well. He was to remain my mentor, and Michael will be helping me a lot in this next stage.

They both rose up to say their goodbyes for now. As they were leaving, Gabriel turned to me and said, "Enjoy your ascendancy!" I asked what that meant or involve. His reply was, "You'll find out. There's a lot to learn."

They finally left.

I remained in a meditative state. Chamuel was laughing and told me that the world is opening to me, and I should be prepared. He agreed I did have a lot to learn, but that I was more than capable of dealing with it. He told me that I was to rouse out soon and that I was the messenger for both angels and the ascended masters now. I had grown beyond the point of no return. They were there for me to pass on their messages, and I was theirs to be their messenger, ally, and friend. The messages I will receive will remain mainly the angels, but the ascended masters will have a say now.

Chamuel told me to rouse out, and I did.

Chamuel is still with me as I write this out and is giving me energy, clarity, and love, for which I am grateful. He has told me that I was to write this out so that others may learn from what happened and how it happened.

Thank you, Chamuel.

***

September 21, 2014

Daily Message from the Angels

Blessed are those who forgive others before themselves. Blessed are those who help others before they help themselves. Blessed are those who love others before they love themselves. Blessed are those who treat others like they themselves would like to be treated. Blessed are those who receive love and give it back threefold. Blessed are those who give unconditionally of themselves to us so that we give ourselves equally. Blessed are those who have accepted a stranger like a brother or sister. Blessed are those who care for each plant and animal as if all life was a priceless treasure.

Yes, you are all blessed in all ways. You have made a difference to others, and they have made a difference to you. There is still much to be done, but each one of you has made a single difference, and when these differences are put together, they make a lot. Keep making differences and make it a task of love. For then it is worth more than jewels.

Be blessed, and you are.

Gabriel

***

September 22, 2014

Daily Message from the Angels

Do you ever wish to be someone other than yourself? Well, why? Is it because they have something you don't have? If that is so, think about this. You may not believe it, but they are probably thinking the same thing about you. You may have something that they don't have.

You may want their money, but what is that? You are rich in your own right, rich in love, rich in knowledge, and rich in spirit.

A perfect body? Well, you have that in spades. You are physically perfect for what your task in life is: to learn. Spiritually, you always were perfect and always will be.

A loving partner? You have your soul mates out there and are just waiting for the right moment. Some will not meet theirs in their current incarnation because of the lesson they must learn now, but they will meet in their next incarnation.

And finally, don't be envious of others and what they have gained. Look at yourself and see what you have gained. You will find that you are more fortunate than you have realised. Is it not so?

Be well, my friends.

Amethyst

***

September 22, 2014

A message that came just a few minutes before, from Angel Adriel.

Times are of the golden type. Many memories are made and rediscovered. Why don't you make a few of your own and make them happy ones at that? Yes, happy memories are the moments when joyful things happen, bringing to you love, laughter, and above all happiness. Your happiness.

Treasure these memories as you make them happen now. They will be of your making, and they will in turn make you. As you make more of these happy moments, you will find that it is infectious. The more people you involve in these moments, the more it will spread out to others. And what is stopping you? The myth that you call society. I agree it is not for all, for each one of you is different in many infinitesimal ways. Yet this society is trying to make you all fit into one shape. That is not the way for any of you. You are, as I said, are all different. Celebrate your uniqueness. Why let others tell you how you should behave.

If you want to smile and be happy when others are frowning, do it! That is your right. If you want to sing a song of joy, do it! If you want to dance in the street, do it! If you want to laugh in joy at the sunshine, do it!

These are your rights and always have been. No one can take them from you, because the Divine gave them to you to use. Those who try to stop you have suppressed their inner joy to the point where it will take a lot to bring it back.

But maybe seeing you may make these people realise what they have hidden within themselves, and maybe they will set themselves free. That is a wonderful vision I have in my mind of what a beautiful sight it would be if everyone was free in spirit and in nature. The music and light that will emanate from you all would be spectacular.

Let your inner child rule and see your world again with such eyes. It was a mysterious and exciting place to be in when a child, full of adventures and play. Make it so again. So much is still yet to be learned, and a lesson that is exciting and full of fun is a lesson that remains permanently in your mind. Learn with that childish excitement, and you will find your tasks will no longer be a chore but a labour of love.

My children, you just heed my words, and you will never go wrong. For you all have that inner child within you, and it is about time you set it free. Stop squashing it and giving out the old excuse that you are too old for childish things. To that I say rubbish! You are never too old. You are in fact letting your responsibilities take too much of your time. You have increased their importance much higher than it is necessary. Downgrade them, please, for such onerous tasks are not that important. Instead, make them fun. If it involves something as minor as a child's drawing on your wall? Make it so. A fun job is a job that is quickly done.

Will you listen, or will you just carry on as normal? That is your choice as always, for I will not interfere with that. Some will carry on with their cheerless lives. For them I feel sadness, but I know that it won't be forever, just delayed.

For those who do listen: Live, enjoy yourselves, be free, sing, dance, and do all sorts of wonderful things. The more joy and happiness that is being created in your life, the more miracles you will see. This is because we are drawn to such feelings. We love to see you happy and want it for all.

Think about this, my children.

Be blessed. I love you.

Adriel

***

September 23, 2014

Daily Message from the Angels

Are you getting enough rest and relaxation in your life? Please tell me you do, for the sake of your physical or mental health. You must rest. Your body depends on that rest to help you heal from your day's events. Your spirit needs the rest to help heal your mind. And your psychic abilities need that rest to help you energize and raise your vibrations.

You all need moments of relaxation, fun, and sleep. These can be called "me times." For the rest moments are for you. Some do hobbies they love. Yes, that is also "me" time. Meditation is "me" time.

But no matter what it is called, it is essential for your physical, mental, and spiritual well-being.

Take your moments of rest and be sure to use them. You all need them, so use them.

Be well.

Serapis Bey

***

September 24, 2014

Daily Message from the Angels

Do you want to know a secret? Well, if so, read on.

The secret that you are to hear is within you. It's called your spirit, your soul, and it is all yours. Your secret is yours to love, to talk with, and to cherish. Your very own secret, and no one else can have it but you.

Want to know something else? There is another aspect of your secret. This is it: we love your secret too, and we love you for keeping that secret close to you. You are our treasure. When the time is right and you have learnt all that you can, then you will find something wonderful.

"What is that?" you ask. "What is that something wonderful?"

Ah, that is our secret.

Be blessed, dear ones.

Michael

***

September 25, 2014

Daily Message from the Angels

Beloved ones, do you not see the beauty that is in front of you? Do you not see how perfect your world is? Do you even see how beautiful you are yourself?

Look and see what is around you. Every little thing that nature gives is for you to love, to care for, and to appreciate. Nature loves you, and nature is beautiful. So why are some people trying to ruin it for others? Only you know yourself, and it is up to you to keep that beauty alive.

Now, as for your own beauty, again some people are trying to ruin that which is your own inner beauty. Don't let them, because they are jealous. They don't see their own beauty, and so they seek to destroy others. Stand up for yourself. Be strong. Be assured that you are beautiful in the Divine's eyes. Be courageous in defending the wonders that nature has given you.

You are all one—don't forget that. You too are nature. You are the children of the Divine, and the Divine lives within you all. Seek, and you shall find.

Be with the Divine.

Ambriel

***

September 26, 2014

Daily Message from the Angels

Believe in yourself, my child. For you can create your own miracles, and you have that power. It is within you and always has been. Don't hide that power away, for it is part of you. Use it.

You can create the miracle of life, and children are the proof. You can create the miracle of music. Just listen to your radio; there is your proof. You can create the miracle of love, and your family and friends are proof.

See? You can create miracles. By the very act of believing in yourself, you can make things happen. There are more miracles within you which I have not listed, but that is for you to find out and explore.

You will never be disappointed in what you see because by then, you will believe in yourself. Aren't you yourself a miracle also?

Think about this, my children.

Be well.

Metatron

***

September 27, 2014

Daily Message from the Angels

Do not hide from yourself, but instead show the world what you are. The Divine made you as you look like now. Therefore, you are perfect. The Divine made your spirit, and that is perfection also. All it needs to do is learn. And in learning, it grows. Let your spirit show itself in your body; let it rule you. You will no longer fear the unknown. You will not hide from others, and you will stand strong among the best of you.

Your spirit is the real you!

Show it, be it, and become it.

Be at peace.

Muriel

***

September 28, 2014

Daily Message from the Angels

There are moments in the universe where one needs to be aware of what is going on around them. There are changes happening right now, and to some they may not appear noticeable, but to others they shine out like a beacon.

There are changes in the growth of your world and the spirit within you. Yes, this is a time of progression and learning. This will happen to all, so don't think you will be missed out, for you won't be.

The energies around you and within the universe are all changing to newer levels. More and more people are becoming aware of new abilities and growing strengths.

You will not be alone in this. It is universal.

Be in peace, beloved ones.

Muriel

***

September 29, 2014

Daily Message from the Angels

There are days of industry and days of rest.

For those days of industry, work well and learn at the same time. This will be the making of you. Do a very good job, and you will earn the respect of your peers and boost your own self-respect.

And on days of rest, let this be a day of fun, recreation, and laughter. Enjoy yourselves to the max. These days are for you alone. We want you to be industrious, but we also want you to be happy and well.

Now, if you have a life that is the combination of both, that is a good balance indeed. If your industry days are also days of fun for you, then you will have achieved harmony in all. That is a step learnt that needs not to be repeated. You have learnt it already, so live it.

Be well, my dear ones.

Michael

***

September 30, 2014

Daily Message from the Angels

Did you know that within you is a very special spark that gave you life? It's a spark that gave you intelligence, a spark that gave you to us. That little spark is a part of the Divine light, and it created you. It will live within you for the infinite lifespan of the universe. It is the very essence of you.

We treasure that spark within you. It is an integral part of you, and you are part of it.

No matter what happens to your body, in many forms of incarnation, that spark remains to be you.

And what is that spark? That spark is your very soul.

Believe in that spark, and believe in yourself, the physical embodiment of that spark.

Be well.

Ariel

***

October 1, 2014

Daily Message from the Angels

No matter what you do, no matter where you are, and no matter who you are, you are loved. That's right. You are loved.

Never feel lonely, unwanted, or sad, because you are loved by us. You will never be forsaken or forgotten. We are always around you.

Yes, you are loved.

Gabriel

***

October 2, 2014

Daily Message from the Angels

Do you remember the days when all was laughter, fun, and many adventures? Those days were your childhood. There were bad memories also, but you don't need those anymore.

It's time to let go of the bad childhood memories, for they no longer serve you and in fact are hindering you. It's time to let go, my dear ones. In letting go, you are opening yourself to greater opportunities that will come your way. Let go of the bad, and you make room in your heart for the good. Let go, dear ones, and bring the light into your life.

I will watch over you during this time.

Uriel

***

October 3, 2014

Daily Message from the Angels

Believe in yourself, for you the one thing in your life that is consistent. The more you believe in yourself, the stronger you become. You will become more than just you—you will become the perfect you.

Your dreams are more likely to become true, your circle of friends will begin to appreciate you more, and your family will begin to realise what a truly wonderful person you are. And it all comes down to you being your true, confident, strong self, just by believing in yourself to be exactly that.

Be well, sweet ones.

Ambriel

***

October 4, 2014

Daily Message from the Angels

Do you believe in magic? Do you?

Have you ever felt the sun on your face and relished the loving warmth on your skin? Have you heard a song that sent shivers down your spine due to the beauty of the sound? Have you seen a rose and admired its innocent beauty? Have you looked in the mirror and appreciated that you are in fact perfect the way you are now? Have you sent us love and received it back threefold?

Do you believe in magic? Yes, all this is magic, and so are you.

Believe!

Serapis Bey

***

October 5, 2014

Daily Message from the Angels

Just sing with your soul. You can do it out loud if you wish, as if the music strokes and lifts your soul. It's a beautiful feeling when that happens. You fly along with the music, and the music becomes your wings. The music of your soul is the life force of all things wonderful. It is part of Creation.

And what is the music of the soul? It is joy. It is happiness. It is beautiful. It is love. It is you!

Let the music happen, and let your love sing through. Be happy, my children, be happy.

Melchizedek

***

October 6, 2014

Daily Message from the Angels

Do you feel the world is against you? As if it is all unfair? Well, think again. The world is not against you at all. It is all open for you, if you let yourself see the open doors.

You don't need to let yourself sink into misery at all. Instead, follow a new path and see what is at the end of it. You may be surprised. When you do this, we will follow you and make sure you never take a step wrong. For this new path was put there for you by us.

As for the "unfair" part, no one ever promised fairness. It is up to you to make your world suit you. If you find yourself blocked from something that you thought you wanted, think again. Maybe it was blocked from you because your path of growth doesn't need it.

You are your own person. You have your free will, and we will follow you wherever your free will takes you, but we will never let you struggle alone. We will never abandon you. But we will never let you fail on your path of growth.

Above all, trust and believe in yourself. You can create your world in any image you want. And you can do this by manifesting.

We will be listening to the entire time.

Believe and be well.

Muriel

***

October 7, 2014

Daily Message from the Angels

Just stop and listen to the world around you. Hear the noise of people and busy traffic. It is hiding the voice of Gaia, and you can't hear her.

Go out to where it is quiet and listen to the whispers that belong to Gaia. She speaks of love, peace, life, and growth. She speaks with the voices of birds, animals, and the wind through trees. She calls you with the moon and with the sun.

Gaia is nature. Gaia is your mother. Gaia is within you all.

Honour your mother, listen to her words, and absorb and heed them. She never speaks of trivia. She speaks of wonders and hope. She is your mother, my dear ones.

Be well.

Ambriel

***

October 8, 2014

Daily Message from the Angels

Just to let you all know: You are loved! The angels love you. The ascended masters love you. Your guides love you. The Divine loves you. We all love you.

So please don't ever think you are unloved, unwanted, and lonely. We are all around you because we love you.

Adriel

***

October 8, 2014

A Message from Archangel Raphael

Believe in us, for we believe in you.

No matter what you have done and no matter what you have said, we believe in you. For in our eyes, you are a child of the Divine, and the Divine's gift is within you. We believe that you—yes, you—are the physical embodiment of that Divine gift.

"What is that gift?" you ask.

The gift is your soul, your spirit, your higher self. The gift has many names, and yet it is only one. But what a gift! It means that the Divine lies within you and will lead you to enlightenment. You can't fight it. In fact, why would you want to? That light is so beautiful and so pure! It is made from pure love, just like you.

Yes! You are made of love, born of love, and are love made into a physical form. This is you. Now, isn't that wonderful? Therefore, we believe in you.

Embrace this beautiful Divine love and let it embrace you back. You will learn to connect with your higher self, and in doing so you will also communicate with us. We await that moment with anticipation because we would love to return your conversation. Though we can hear you, very few can hear us. This can be frustrating for you, we know. But it isn't for forever.

We also hear and see your thoughts and dreams. We can interact with you there, but you rarely remember us. Your soul does remember, though. It remembers us perfectly well, and so it will filter our words and instructions to you.

There are a few of you asking about times where there are changes happening. It has happened! Now is the time for you all to relearn what was lost and discover what is new. Learn well, dear ones. Learn well.

You are the future of your new world, and you must let go and leave the past behind; you no longer need it, and it will no longer serve a purpose for you. Grow, learn, discover, and be the future. After all, the future is all for you.

The changes that will happen will be gradual and will depend on our lightworkers. They will awaken what Divine light that is within you. The lightworkers are the beacons that will guide you to us. They have many skills.

Some are lightwarriors. They will fight for you and are on our side. They are the ones who have the courage to face and fight the darkness.

There are the heralds. They pass our messages via writing and by voice. They give out the words of Divine voice—our words and the Divine's.

There are the beacons. They will guide the lost into the light. Their presence is of comfort and love. They will light your way so that you won't stumble or fall off your path.

There are the light bearers. They will provide the source and the love to bring you further into the light. They will bring your skills to the forefront. They are the priests and priestesses.

There are the healers. If your light has been damaged by the darkness, they shall repair the damage it has caused. They will replace lost energy. They are pure inside in many ways.

There are the mentors. They are the born teachers. They will teach you to grow further and beyond your limits. They will teach you to grow to the point where you too will become the next group of lightworkers.

Yet these people are not restricted in one ability. A lightwarrior can also be a beacon. A mentor can also be a healer and a herald. You are not restricted and never will be. You will be free to swing from one to another.

Some lightworkers, especially the heralds, shall work with us. We will show them their paths and give them the knowledge of what is required next. But note this: we are not restricted to the heralds. You too will be working with us.

That is wonderful! That is perfect! That is meant to be!

Take note, my dear ones. We are always watching you, loving you, and encouraging you along your path to us.

That is all I need to say, for any more is surplus.

Be well, my dear ones, be well.

Raphael

***

October 9, 2014

Daily Message from the Angels

My darling ones, you who have so many wonders waiting for you in your future know so little of what will happen when you find them. Well, do not worry. What will happen is that you will grow in knowledge. You will find yourself surrounded by all-encompassing love, and the music of the stars will sing for you. Your world will become a rainbow of joy, happiness, compassion, and love.

This is what your future holds for you. You may incarnate a few more lifetimes before you reach this, but no matter what, you will get there. And it will be waiting for you.

We will be waiting for you with open arms.

It is so beautiful, and so are you.

Gabriel

***

October 10, 2014

Daily Message from the Angels

Just remember where you are going, my friends.

You are going to a new future. Forget the past; it has served its purpose and is finished with. Now is the time to go forward and into your own future.

You have the world before you, ready for you to take your first steps in it. You can create your own world just by being in it. And your actions show which path your own world will take. Take a path of sadness and anger, and your own world will reflect this. And that will be all you ever experience in it.

But if you take a path of happiness, joy, compassion, and love, then you will experience a path and a future full of such in return.

Now, do you remember what path you are taking?

Think about this, my friends.

Emmanuel

***

October 11, 2014

Daily Message from the Angels

Just imagine! What if you knew your own future step by step? And that you knew where it would end? Would you still live your life as it is now?

I don't think you would.

You are not meant to know your future in the years ahead. That is because you constantly change it day by day. Sure, knowing your future within the next few months with general terms is OK. That is accepted. But in detail, it is not. It is not because it is forbidden but because you change it with every decision you make.

Besides, wouldn't your life be boring if you knew first-hand what the details are? Leave that to us. We know what your future will be, and we will make sure that it happens in the direction it is supposed to go. Leave us with the petty details. All you need to do is enjoy yourself and live for the moment.

Be well, dear ones.

Jeremiel

***

October 12, 2014

Daily Message from the Angels

Do as you wish, but don't harm others in doing so. That is one of the great laws of the universe. It is also the law of karma and destiny.

Treat others the same way you wish to be treated. That way you can be assured of peace and good karma. That is also a way to your inner peace. If it feels right deep within you, then it is so.

Choose wisely your friends, because you can't choose your relatives. That is also one of the laws. This is showing that you are not your relatives, but an individual of your own self with your own ideas and spirit. You are not your relatives. Do you hear me? If there are some relatives who could drag you down, don't let them and move away from them. You are you, and they are themselves. You are not the same.

Be yourself, be true, and believe in your very own self. That is what is meant to be. Trust your own instincts and be prepared to follow them. They will never lead you wrong, for they are a sign that your guides are working with you.

Believe in yourself!

Galadiel

***

October 13, 2014

Daily Message from the Angels

Let go of the hurts of the past. Let them go, and you will no longer be haunted by them. They will no longer own you because you will be finally free. Do honour yourself with a feeling of freedom and joy as the ties of the past are finally released.

You will be free. You will be flying. You will be happy.

Don't let the past destroy you. What is past is past and can no longer hurt you. Let go of the memories; they are what are hurting you. They are what are keeping you from being free again.

Memories are just that, memories. The situation of the memory is no longer existing. Let it go and be free like the birds, soaring in the sky and enjoying the wind beneath their wings. Let the wind be beneath your wings, and fly.

Tiriel

***

October 14, 2014

Daily Message from the Angels

Believe in the beauty of the universe. It is there and all around you. Believe in the beauty of nature. It is there also, and you are one of the many manifestations of it. Believe in the miracles of angels, for you are surrounded by them. Believe in the wonderful Divine; the Divine made you with love. Believe in love, because that is what makes the world go around. Believe in yourself, for you are perfect in the eyes of the Divine and us.

Do you see the common theme, my friends?

Believe!

We believe in you!

Sananda Jesus

***

October 15, 2014

Daily Message from the Angels

Be sweet within you, for all the good sweetness that dwells within you is of the purest love. It is Divine, it is wonderful, and it is true!

As you hold that sweetness within you, you will find that there will be wonders around you. Have seen the sunrise? The beautiful colours it can create? That is one of the wonders that the Divine has given to you.

"What is this sweetness within you?" some say. It is your very spirit, your soul, your Divine light. Treasure this beautiful gift, for it is the very essence of you and is the Divine in you.

Be well, sweet ones.

Ariel

***

October 16, 2014

Daily Message from the Angels (In This Case, My Spirit Guide)

Let all those who belong to this world look towards the light. For the light is there and waiting for you to let it into your life.

You who are waiting for this light, wait no more. It is here and always will be. You who are trying to hide from it, give up! You cannot hide from the Divine light, for it can see you wherever you go, no matter how deep you go underground.

You who have already embraced the light and accepted it within you, you are now blessed and will be blessed further. You who are standing and about to receive this light, expect miracles into your life. You are to be blessed.

The Divine light is a blessing to you all, and no darkness can win against it. The Divine light is purity, happiness, joy, and beauty.

The Divine light is the Divine. You are part of this great design in the Divine's plan for the universe.

Amaru

***

October 17, 2014

Daily Message from the Angels

Are you ready for your next great adventure called life? Are you ready?

Are you ready to stand up for your own rights? Are you ready to learn new and wonderful things? Are you ready to experience miracles? Are you ready to evolve?

If so, then seek the light within you. Seek the wonders of the universe that lie inside.

My dearest ones, you are made of the light and born of the light. You are one with the universe, and the universe lies within you. You are all interconnected. When will you realise you cannot be apart from something that is an integral part of you?

You were made for the specific purpose to grow, develop, and become guardians of the light.

Lightworkers all, you will be so.

Listen well.

Balthazar

***

October 18, 2014

Daily Message from the Angels

Beloved ones, hear my call.

I call the lightworkers of your world, to come forward and bring the Divine light fully onto everyone in your world.

Now is the time when the energies are high, and you all need to bring this light from the Divine, so that others may turn to it and be in sight of the Divine. This is necessary so that all darkness and negativity can be removed, purifying your world.

Bring that Divine light and surround your planet with it. It is healing, loving, and uplifting. And Gaia needs it to happen too. Bring it forth, dear ones. Bring it forth.

Be well.

Barachiel

***

October 19, 2014

Daily Message from the Angels

Let us try something different.

Why don't you all find a spot where you can be undisturbed and relax totally?

Sit comfortably there, relax, and let your mind go deep within.

Sink deeper still until you find yourself with the sensation of floating.

As you feel this, visualise a bright pale blue star and place it in the very centre of your being.

Do you see it?

Now visualise your "soul" fingers reaching forward and touching it.

When you do this, direct love towards that star via your fingers.

Now watch what happens, because you will like this.

It is beautiful, and in doing this, you are sending love to your very inner core of you. And it is that which also hosts the spark from the Divine.

Enjoy what happens.

Be well.

Jehudiel

***

October 20, 2014

Daily Message from the Angels

Why don't you all stop and listen to the sounds of nature.

The birds, the wind, and even the trickle of raindrops. Such is always ignored by everyone, yet it is ever there. These sounds are the voice of your world. Listen, and hear the life surge deep under the ground; feel the energy of growth ripple through the soil.

You need this world, and it needs you. By touching the ground with your fingers or feet, you are feeding your soul and neutralizing any negative energies. You call it grounding. I call it getting in touch with nature.

Hear the voice of your world; it whispers to you all the time.

Be well, my sweet ones.

Ambriel

***

October 21, 2014

Daily Message from the Angels

When you wish to develop and grow, remember this: meditate! It helps you to connect with us at a higher level, which is beneficial to you.

Even when you just too busy, just remember the golden light of the Divine is still around you. Whether you meditate or not, it is there.

Meditation brings you a much bigger and stronger flow to you though, and when that happens, you can bathe in it if you want. It is there for you and is freely given. It is given in love, and the golden light of the Divine surrounds you. Take as much of it as you want, for it is eternal and limitless.

You can't have too much or too little.

Think about it.

Michael

***

October 22, 2014

Daily Message from the Angels

You think this is a harsh, cold world, and you are in the middle of it. Wrong!

It is a beautiful world with many flowers, oceans, insects, birds, and beasts. Each is unique. They are placed in this world to experience life and learn. They too will grow within.

It is you who have closed your eyes to your world and let in the darkness. It is you who made your own perception of the world real to you. And it is you who can change it.

Take a few minutes a day to look at something beautiful, even if it is a little daisy on the lawn. Take those few minutes to appreciate simple beauty. Then gradually expand that time and see more beauty around you. You will never be disappointed, but you will be surprised.

Let that little ray of light enter you with this pleasurable experience. As you grow with the beauty, the beauty that is the light grows within.

Never lock yourself away from your world, for you cannot hide from it. It is always there, just like us. Please appreciate your world.

And the ultimate revelation when you get to appreciate all this beautiful world of yours and come to love it? It is that you too are part of this world. You too are beautiful.

Be well, dear ones, and learn.

Melchizedek

***

October 23, 2014

Daily Message from the Angels:

Do you ever get those days where you just want to dance or sing? Well, do it!

You want to have fun, and by all rights you deserve it. Have fun! Enjoy the moment.

We love seeing you like this. It means that your spirit is happy, and so are you. It is as it should be. Life is for having fun, enjoyment, and happiness.

You can create your own happiness out of seemingly nothing, but there is substance. The energy that you give off during your happy moments is seen by the Divine and us, and it shines so brightly.

It pleases us all. We want you to be happy. That is the most direct path to enlightenment. Happiness raises your energies so much that you are a beacon to us. We come, we see your energy, and we encourage your happiness by adding our love.

Be happy and be free. Above all, if you want to dance, then dance. Do you want to sing out loud? Do it! No matter how flat your voice is, it is what is making you happy. That is more important. Sing, my songbirds. Sing.

Be well, my beloved children.

Michael

***

October 24, 2014

Daily Message from the Angels (In This Case, an Ascended Master)

For what are you all waiting for? Are you waiting for a surprise? Are you waiting for love? Are you waiting for an opportunity to knock?

Well, stop waiting. If you sit there and just wait, it will never come to you. You must go out and seek it out, for it waits for you.

That surprise? Don't sit back for it. Ask us to arrange one for you, no matter what for it is, and then walk out the door into an adventure. Your wonderful surprise will come to you, but in a form you never expect.

Love? Get off your rear and go outside to look for it. It may be right there, waiting for you. Possibly around the next corner or even at a place you least expect it.

Opportunity? Yes, go places where such opportunities exist. There may be an opening for you there. You must seek it out and ask for it.

Yes, you know the saying: "God helps those who help themselves." This is what it means. Get out in your big, wide world and help yourself. We will help you on your way.

Be well.

Merlin

***

October 25, 2014

Daily Message from the Angels

Beloved ones, rejoice in the beauty of your inner selves. You are unique, every single one of you. Even identical twins have something unique in them. Rejoice in your individuality, for it means you are a free person and you are strong. Don't worry about what others say to you about this. This is your life, not theirs.

Live like you are supposed to live: free, joyful, and with love.

You are, after all, one of the Divine lights.

Be well, my dear ones, be well.

Emmanuel

***

October 26, 2014

Daily Message from the Angels

Let us now rejoice. For now, is the time that big changes are to be made in your world. You too have the voice to name changes you want. You too have the power to help.

Do you want more love for everyone? It is available for you all to use; it is out there waiting for you to reach forward and take.

You want the oceans to be free of pollution? That is also something you can do. Reach out and clear it up simply by using the power of you!

You have the power to change your own world. You can use it to change negativity to positivity. This is all part of your gift of free will. It is also your gift of manifesting. You have always had it but never used it. Well, that time is now. You now know it and can use it. Do so and be amazed at what changes one little word can do.

Reach forward and take what is given to you, dear ones. It was given to you all as a gift. Take your gift and be thankful. For it is a gift beyond measure.

It is the gift called free will.

Be well, sweet ones.

Michael

***

October 27, 2014

Daily Message from the Angels

Do you wonder at what lies above you in the stars? Do you feel a need to explore that great expanse of flickering lights? Don't hide away from that curiosity and need to know, for it was put there for you to learn with.

The stars above belong to many suns, and each one of them is part of you. As you are part of the universe, the universe is also a part of you. The same energies and matter that made those galaxies made you. The Divine made them and you with one single thought.

You are special indeed.

Be well within yourselves.

Gabriel

***

October 28, 2014

Daily Message from the Angels

Just relax; that is all you need to do. Any stress or problem that comes into your life is a mere nothing. The more you relax and settle into a deeper state of mind, the quicker your body and mind will begin to heal. This too will help you all to develop further on your path.

Stresses will drag you down, and you don't need that, especially when it appears that the problem is a mere nothing.

If the problem gets too much, leave it. Call upon us to shoulder it; we can do this quite easily, and we have abilities to make things happen that you don't have.

Never waste your power on something that doesn't merit it. Instead, let us deal with the situation; you deal with loving yourself.

We mention this with love and hope that you will grow.

Be strong and be well, sweet ones.

Gabriel

***

October 29, 2014

Daily Message from the Angels

Let those who are at your side, be within your heart. Let those who listen to you without prejudice be listened to back with an open heart. Let those who laugh with you with truth in their hearts be with you in your memories. Let those who stand side by side with you in times of adversity be your constant companions in times of peace. Let those who stand up against negativity in support of you be yours in all loyalty. Let the truth be shown that all the strong should treasure those who are weak. For even the weakest of persons has strength in many other ways that can outdo the apparently strongest.

Be true to each other. Respect each other, and above all be there for each other. For you are beautiful apart, but you are perfection together. Be sharing in your heart and joy, for they will be returned to you threefold. Karma can be vicious to those who abuse it, but very loving and tender to those who respect it.

Let it be so, my dear ones, let it be so.

I wish you well on your journey to enlightenment.

Ambriel

***

October 30, 2014

Daily Message from the Angels

Your actions define what you are. You destroy someone's dream; you will find yourself spiritually damaged in turn. You harm someone, and you will be morally harmed back.

It also works the other way around.

You give someone hope to live for; you will receive much hope back. You help someone who is hurt; you will receive their love back. You provide support for someone who has fallen; you will be supported back when it is your turn.

This is the way it is meant to be. Be the one who helps and gives willingly. In turn, you will receive much love and more.

This is the way it is meant to be. Be that special someone.

I see you, I hear you, and I feel you.

Raziel

***

October 31, 2014

Daily Message from the Angels

Wonderful people, treasures you are.

You who have given love to others and received it back. You are the parents, you are the children, and you are the lovers.

Love is a beautiful thing, and it spreads like the fire on dry grass. Let it burn within you, and let it spread from you to beyond the stars.

You are all treasured by the one who gave you this love. It is within you and others. Share it, experience it, and live it. It is what has made you, and you have made it in return.

Feel the glow and joy of it. It is far more precious than any drug or alcoholic drink, and it lasts a lot longer too—in fact for years.

Remember where this love is: in you.

Share it please and be receiving it back. It is all worth it now and in the end.

Be well.

Amnediel

***

November 1, 2014

Daily Message from the Angels:

Let go, let God, and let love. Such easy and simple words that mean so much, for they are the words towards enlightenment and truth. It is a beautiful moment when you live those words. Miracles happen, and why not? After all, you are a miracle yourself—a miracle called life. Do it! Live it! Be it!

What a wonderful experience it is.

Be well.

Gabriel

***

November 2, 2014

Daily Message from the Angels

Go forward, my beloved ones. Go forward in life. There is a great new future for you all, and it is all-empowering.

Don't back away and be left behind. Instead, join with us all and become enlightened. Become with the light and be with our love.

Don't run away, for you will just stumble. When that happens, we will come to you and try to help you. And in that, we ask you to come with us. If you still turn us down, it will sadden us, but we won't let you be alone. We will stay with you.

Don't hide from your future. In fact, you can't because it follows you around.

Don't forget other friends and family because they may want to take that wonderful journey, and they also want you to join them.

The Divine sees all. The Divine hears all. The Divine does not want you to miss out on this.

Step forward, join with everyone else on your new path to your glorious future, and watch the world open for you.

Be well.

Gabriel

***

November 3, 2014

Daily Message from the Angels

Yes, it is that time when I shall show my works to you all. It is the time for you all to heed the words of the One.

Hold your love inside of your heart, for it is precious and much desired by the darkness. Keep your heart sealed from those who will take what your light is. For those who try and remove that light from you, step back and let the words of denial flow from your lips. Call upon the angels to help you defend your gift of light and grace. It is yours, not of the darkness.

Back off from those who offer temptations to the darkness. For that is not the way; it is instead the path to nowhere.

I shall provide the path to the light; I shall provide the path to the Divine. I am the one who will provide all this. I am the one who treasures that light within you. I am the one who will help you protect it. I am the one who gave that light to all.

I am the One.

No name was left. After this message, I broke down and cried. This went on for five minutes, and then it suddenly stopped as quickly as it started. The entire time, I felt no urge to cry, and I mentally called out, asking what was going on. Michael came through and told me not to worry. He kept giving me encouragement.

***

November 4, 2014

Daily Message from the Angels

Do you believe in magic? The magic that apparently comes from nowhere, and infiltrates the world with wonders and beauty? If you do, then well done! You have seen what we see all the time in your world. It is you!

If you don't, then you are missing out the most wondrous of the many gifts the Divine has given you. It is the magic of life, love, joy, miracles, nature, and above all you! To deny that magic, you deny the very essence of you. You were created by the Divine, who used this "magic" and installed it within you.

The Divine is the magic. The Divine is within you all. You are all magic. Blessed ones, never undersell yourselves. You are more beautiful than you believe.

Be well.

Michael

***

November 5, 2014

Daily Message from the Angels

Breathe in the fresh air of the new day. Breathe deeply and thank the Divine for that moment. Such is that moment that it is reminiscent of the first breath you took on arrival on your world. It is a breath of new beginnings, a new start and a new promise of your future. Such as it is every morning, such as it is with the day you were born. All new starts and futures. That is such a wonderful thing, and it is so precious.

Remember that with such new starts, you can create your own promises to the light. Enjoy the moment and ask the golden light of the Divine to shine on you. Then take that deep breath of the golden light, and let it infuse you with its love.

There is no better protection; there is no better love.

Be well.

Cassiel

***

November 6, 2014

Daily Message from the Angels

Believe in yourself first, and when you do that, that's when you become the miracle you originally are. Once it is installed into you that you are the most important thing in your life, that's when you realise that your love is beyond infinity and can include others with you.

You can love hundreds or thousands of people and still have room for more. This is because you are a receptacle of love, and regarding he love you give out to those others, expect it back many times, for it is self-sustaining.

Give your love freely and without any catches or expectations, and you will be rewarded many times. We love you without any such hindrances, and our reward is to see you love yourself and us.

Be well, sweet ones.

Daniel

***

November 7, 2014

Daily Message from the Angels

Let your Light be your Love Light.
Let your heart be open to another person's love.
Let your mind be open to the words of wisdom and enlightenment.
Let your soul be purified by the Divine.
Let your path be as smooth as the golden light that shines on you.
Let your eyes see the wonders of the universe.
Let your beliefs be as beautiful as the rainbow.
Let your words speak of Divine wisdom.
Let your body work in the name of love and beauty.
Let your feet walk to the Divine sight.
Let yourself be the example of pure love and light.
Let yourself be.

Be so, and you will find that nothing can stop you; nothing would want to. For in becoming so, you are becoming nearer to the beautiful and perfect truth. Let it happen.

I am yours in such wonders.

Gabriel

***

November 8, 2014

Daily Message from the Angels

What a wonderful world you have. There is such beauty in its very forests and fields. The birds within sing their joy to us. Why don't you sing your joy to us also? We will hear and be joyous with you. We will listen with our own hearts, and likely be singing with you. Sing your love, sing your praises, and above all sing your souls.

Such beauty in your voices should never be ignored, and it will not be ignored by us. We want to hear from you, and we want to be singing with you.

Sing with your voice of love and joy. Raise your voices and sing to us.

"What is the music you shall sing to?" some of you ask. Why, it is the very music of your own love. Sing your love, and let love sing to all.

Be well and believe.

Michael

***

November 9, 2014

Daily Message from the Angels

Do in this world exactly as you wish but remember what you do will come back to you threefold.

You give others your love freely; expect it back three-fold.

You give someone in need a much-needed helping hand; be prepared to have someone help you out even further when you fall.

You love a child that is not yours with unconditional love and protection; your guardian angels will return that love to you with much more power behind it.

You give without asking; expect a bigger gift back.

All this if you do freely and with love; expect three times that love back and in many forms.

This is called karma. And karma works in many ways, for karma is a teacher.

Be well, sweet ones. I shall await your responses in love and karma.

Cassiel

***

November 10, 2014

Daily Message from the Angels

At last. It is now time for you all to be aware of us. Time for you to grow and become more than just travellers on your planet, but to travel beyond your world and into the universe.

Your world is just one living spacecraft for your current forms, but time has come for your world to grow beyond its current sphere of existence. You are in this world; you too will grow with your world.

Grow, learn, and grow more. It is all part of the cycle of the universe.

Enlightenment is part of the Divine promise for you.

Yes, we have plans for you all—every single one of you. And it is magnificent. Those who have reached beyond enlightenment and have now ascended: your tasks have just begun. You are to be the bringers of the light within everyone.

You will help the children grow within the light and help them embrace us within their souls. Ascended ones, you are more than just lightworkers; you are part of the source.

I hear you all; I see you all.

Well done.

Emmanuel

***

November 11, 2014

Daily Message from the Angels

I see the stars that shine around your world. Such beauty can only be from the Divine's own hand. Such wonders that occur within your world are also by the Divine's own hand.

Your world is one of the wonders. The plants are another. The beasts that walk, fly, and swim on your world—them too. Your sun. Your moon. They too are such wonders.

You? Yes, you! You are one of the many wonders also, but a very special wonder indeed. You have the knowledge and the ability to join with the love of the Divine. You can cure your own world or destroy it.

Please choose to heal the world, for it is all you have.

You are made from the Divine's own hands, and you have the Divine's gift of healing.

The choice is yours.

Be blessed.

Damabiah

***

November 12, 2014

Daily Message from the Angels

Blessed ones. You know of the happenings in your world. Well, we have noticed this long ago, and we have also noticed the cause.

The Divine is of no religion. The Divine is the Divine itself. We are not Catholic. We are not Muslim or Jewish. We are what we are: pure love and Divine presence. We serve no other being but the Divine, and the Divine's will be our will also.

The Divine wants the fighting to stop, so do we. We will always obey the Divine first and foremost. We all want you to stop the fighting. Learn to see within yourself and hold your head down in shame, for we did not want you to fight among yourselves. We wanted you to be in joy, peace, and love. Learn to love and live. We want you to do that instead.

There is so much going on in your world that the only way you can redeem yourselves is by embracing love, not war.

Be with love.

Ashtar

***

November 13, 2014

Daily Message from the Angels

Let your soul rest in the glowing gold light of the Divine. Bathe your body in this light and feel its energies infuse with you. Welcome that light into your life and let it be part of you. Let you become part of it in return. This light is from the Divine, and it is freely available for you to absorb, breathe, and bathe in.

What is this light? It is called love.

Now, let it become you. Take as much as you want or need; it is a never-ending supply. It will never run out. It is pure, unconditional love.

Be well.

Matthias

***

November 14, 2014

Daily Message from the Angels

Do you realise what you can do now? Do you know what amazing powers you have at your fingertips?

You have the whole world in front of you, and it can be accessed from within your very own soul.

You are powerful, you are a tower of strength, and you are wonderful. You can do this because you can. You are that special person with that special gift.

The words of wisdom are within you, and you can speak them now. You can let the world know your skills, words, and harmony. You are the words; you are the wisdom; you are of the light.

Speak now, and never let others stop you.

You are beautiful.

Raziel

***

November 15, 2014

Daily Message from the Angels and Ascended Masters

Let none take your grandness away from you. Do not let anyone try to steal it or destroy it. For it is yours alone, and none other shall touch it. Do not even let those people near you, for they will feed off your energy and try to repress you to their idea as to what you should be. That is not the way it is meant to be.

What is meant to be is your freedom, your happiness, and your own personal individuality. They are what make you powerful and strong. Nurture your own power and uniqueness, for they are yours alone to own and cherish. These are your strengths and will forever remain so.

You are all children of the light, and each of you is a special gift from the Divine to your world. You are all such magnificent creatures, so never let lower energy try to own you. For that path is a path of sadness, self-destruction, and illness.

Be free, be yourself, and be the best you can be. For you can only grow better if you do that. Grab your beautiful future and leave the past behind.

Let it be so.

Emmanuel

***

November 16, 2014

Daily Message from the Angels and Ascended Masters

Just who do you think you are? Do you think you are the centre of the universe and the stars? No! The Divine is at the centre and created the universe.

You are one of the many lights that the Divine has sent out to experience this life in your world. You are not the centre of any universe. You *are* the universe.

Because you are of the Divine light, you are made with what the universe is also made of. The Divine partly resides in every single one of you, seeing and experiencing what you do. You *are* the universe.

The Divine created the universe; the Divine created you. You are a child of the stars, the child of light, and the child of the Divine. We are kin.

Be well, my little siblings.

Gabriel

***

November 17, 2014

Daily Message from the Angels and Ascended Masters

Let love be your guiding light. Let it lead you to the pureness and beauty that is within all of you. It is part of what makes you so beautiful.

Love is part of the Divine will and the Divine light. It is deep within you. Never ignore it or fob it off as if it was a mere emotion that can be squashed and hidden away. All that does is bring you down. But despite that, you cannot escape it. Love will seek and find you; it will drag you out kicking and screaming into the light.

You can't hide from love, for it is always deep within you. It finds a way out, and you can't stop it. So why not just relax and accept it for what it is: Divine will.

Be blessed and be with love.

Gabriel

***

November 18, 2014

Daily Message from the Angels and Ascended Masters

Beloved ones, why do you worry so much? Is not your world a beautiful one? Are you not loved by us? Are you not loved by our mutual parent, the Divine?

Your worries are really of your own making. You are all making a small problem become a bigger one by stressing about it.

Do you have financial difficulties? No problem; give us that worry of yours and trust in us. We will fix it. All you must do is love us, tell us in detail what the problem is, and show us with your mind the situation cured.

All we need is you. All you need is us. We need each other, my dear ones. For we have each other to love and cherish. We are one in many aspects— in love, in our mutual parent, and in the light.

Trust us, relax, and let in the Divine into your life. Let it be so, beloved ones.

We await your response.

Raphael

***

November 19, 2014

Daily Message from the Angels and Ascended Masters

Just look at what is within yourself.

The love light which glows within you? That belongs to the One.
The stars in your eyes? They belong to the One.
The emotions and laughter? They belong to the One.
Your very thoughts and breath? They belong to the One.
You belong to the One.

The One created you and loved you. The One gave you free will in order that you may grow and learn. In doing so, you may be nearer to the One, like a child and parent. The One lies within you all, for is not your very soul made by the One also?
You are a child of the universe, and the universe was made by the One.

Star child, grow and become of the light.

The One awaits your presence with love and kindness.

That is meant to be.

I am the One.

***

November 20, 2014

Daily Message from the Angels and Ascended Masters

Believe me when I say you are rushing forward into a new destiny—a destiny that will bring enlightenment, and truth to you all. You may experience this in your current lifetime or the next. But whatever your direction is, you are heading to your ultimate form. That is the form of light, of futures and pasts that have merged into one. You are the future of your own world.

And what will you look like in this form?

You will be more beautiful than you are now. You will have no need of any physical restrictions. In fact, you will be free of illness, pain, and sadness. Above all, you can fly.

Your true self is the most beautiful thing in your world. It shines with the purest light of truth and love. You will be the colours of the rainbow. This is the future of you all. You were made from stars, and you will take your place amongst them as star children.

Worthy indeed. You are that. Your ascended masters have made that journey, and they are star children.

My children of light hear my words and learn. Nothing is static, nothing is immovable, and nothing is impossible.

Go forward, upwards, and outwards. Shine your light and fly free.

Jeremiel

***

November 21, 2014

Daily Message from the Angels and Ascended Masters

Do you realise how special you all are?

Your world flies through the universe at high speed, and you reside in this world. You should call it Spaceship Earth in reality. After all, is it not a living craft taking you into the depths of the universe?

You have created your own world to survive in, and then you are slowly hurting it. Stop, look around you, and accept the fact that your world was perfect in the beginning. You must not change perfection, but you can enhance it.

You are the guardians of your world, and so you must look after it. You must protect your world from harm. This includes taking responsibilities for your own actions. No blaming others for your own mistakes. Fix what you have destroyed, and above all heal what life has been harmed.

You are the guardians of your world—act like it and be them! Then hold your head high in pride at a job well done. You will soon find that quite a few problems in your world will suddenly disappear if your world is properly looked after.

Guardians do your duty and do it well.

Gabriel

***

November 22, 2014

Daily Message from the Angels and Ascended Masters:

Just remember how wonderful you are. Don't forget it whatever happens. You are amazing and beautiful, and we believe you should know it. Remember the laughter in your life and love. That memory is a gift to you. Treasure it.

As your world changes and goes through its different phases, you must remember the positive side of you. The side that we love most of all. The side that is of the light and is full of joy. This is the side we want to see more of in you. As your world changes, so will you. These changes will enhance that light side if it is dominant. So keep positive thoughts and live them.

If you let the negativity in your life rule you, you won't be able to change and will get left behind. Growth is meant to be for everyone; please don't let negativity make you reject that beautiful gift.

Open your hearts to it and absorb the love of the Divine.

I hear you and see you.

Be in the light.

Emmanuel

***

November 23, 2014

Daily Message from the Angels and Ascended Masters

As one little seed grows, it takes on a life of its own. Each leaf is an extension of its own body. It gets stronger with each passing moment in time, and in the end, it results in the bud that will open, showing its face to the world and spreading its seeds out to others.

Such is my channel. She has started as a seedling with grew in time, and each of her leaves was her experiences and gifts towards life. As she has become enlightened, she has budded out. Now she has flowered through the light within her, her words are the future seeds of wisdom and growth.

It is the same for you all. You are the seeds, plants, and flowers of the future. You have the words of light within you and always will have, for they are the Divine's words. And as it should be, for my channel is still growing, spreading out further roots into both worlds. Soon it will be the same for you all. Learn, grow, blossom, and spread the seeds of wisdom and light.

Never be afraid of us, for we will never harm you.

Be well, my beloved ones, be well.

Michael

***

November 24, 2014

Daily Message from the Angels and Ascended Masters

Let go of what does not serve you, for it now belongs to the past. The past cannot come back, and it no longer exists in your world.

Let go of old hurts, grudges, and emotional pain. Time to wipe your slate clean, ready for your future.

Let go of what is holding you back and let go of those people who try to stop you from going forward. They too belong to the past and should be removed from your life. Let them linger behind, but don't let them take you with them. They do not have that right and never will have.

Instead, clear out the garbage that ties you down and begin to take a step forward into your future with an unburdened heart. Have a soul that is free and unencumbered with life's past spoils.

Be free and fly into the sky.

Be well.

Ambrose

***

November 25, 2014

Daily Message from the Angels and Ascended Masters

Let your own self be in the space of quietude and solitary. Take yourself to that spot where you will not be disturbed, and you will find peace.

Now in that space, sit down and relax. Close your eyes and listen to your breathing. Feel how it works through your body.

Now visualise that you have been surrounded by golden light and breathe in that light. Feel it go through your very own body and go through to each cell, energising and cleansing.

You are at that stage, glowing with this golden light also because it is bathing you. Now form a small ball of pink light in your heart the colour of the rose quartz. As soon as you feel that the pink energy orb in your heart is the size of a fist and pulsating, send it to the source of the golden light.

What you have done is an exchange of love. The Divine loves you with its golden light, and you have shown the Divine your love with a pink rose light.

The exchange of love energy has a very interesting side effect. Expect to find the golden light to intensify for a short while. This is not dangerous but beautiful, for it is the Divine giving you more love for the gift you gave.

During this interchange, you can directly speak to the Divine. The Divine will hear. As for the Divine's answers, you shall feel them deep within your soul, and you will subconsciously know the reply.

Dearest ones, this is a gift from me to you—the gift of the love exchange. Use it wisely and as often as you wish. For it is free, just like the golden light.

I thank you, my dear ones.

Emmanuel

***

November 26, 2014

Daily Message from the Angels and Ascended Masters

Just one breath. That's all it needs.
One breath to take in the energies of the Divine.
One breath to start a new life.
One breath to start a word.
One breath to end a problem.
One breath to create a song.
One breath to close an open door.
One breath to begin a promise.
One breath to bring new hope.
One breath to live again.
One breath to call for us.
One breath to say, "I love you."
One breath to say, "I care."

That's all that is required. For everything in this universe has its starting point, and so do you. All you need is that one breath to start things new.

Breathe, and create.

Michael

***

November 27, 2014

Daily Message from the Angels and Ascended Masters

Now is the time to open your hearts to us. We have been waiting for such a long time for you to turn and call us to you. You see, things are happening in your world, and we can make this change easy for you. Just call us to help. The change that your world is going through has been planned since the time of Creation. You will change with it. Just open your heart and mind to the Divine and us. Those who do not and reject us: that is your free will, but it means we cannot help you as you refused our help. They will get delayed. But once they finally turn to us to help, we will be there to give that help. Our patience is infinite, and we are always willing to help.

I agree we do meddle at times, but it is for your own good. When you find yourself on a path you don't think is right, but suddenly find yourself turning a different corner, that is us. We want you to stay on your true path. We select the people you should meet that can help you. But you can also meet those of your own choosing too. Your choice again, your free will.

Accept our offer of help during this transition to higher vibrations. We can make it much easier for you.

Be well.

Ambriel

***

November 28, 2014

Daily Message from the Angels and Ascended Masters:

Love the Divine! Love us! Love each other! Love yourself!

The four most important rules in your life. There is nothing more important than those four rules. After all, without love, all of us will be lost. You live with love, work with love, breathe in love, and are made with love. And from love you came, and with love you live. When the time has come of partings, you go back to the love you came from.

The cycle of life should also be called the cycle of love. We all go through with it. We are all part of it. Accept what is rightfully yours to take: love! Yes, there is more to come. In fact, there is no shortage, and that is a good thing. Feel it, speak it, know it, belong to it, and be it. All is one, and the One is all.

It is there for you all.

Be well.

Michael

***

November 29, 2014

Daily Message from the Angels and Ascended Masters:

Do not let tears destroy what wonders you have received. Instead, let them cleanse you. Don't see them as sadness, but instead see them as removing the stresses and negativity from you. Don't cry because of the problems you have. Instead, face the problem and fight back. Nothing is worth being sad about.

A heart that is broken is not worth the tears. Just move on and let things go. If it's broken, then it wasn't for you anyway. Instead, move on to something better that is meant for you.

If a person who has caused you so much stress and a lot worry, don't cry on that. Instead, use the easiest solution: remove the problem.

You see, nothing is worth the tears. Instead, save them for the moments you need to cleanse yourself. When your body wishes to remove such negative energy, it makes you grow tears.

Once that is done, change those cleansing tears and replace them with tears of joy. Let them bring back the joy into your life, dear one. You have much more to offer than you ever know. So instead, no sad tears, just cleaning tears.

Once gone, let the joy into your life. You will feel so much refreshed.

Be well.

Chamuel

***

November 30, 2014

Daily Message from the Angels and Ascended Masters

As the night approaches, let yourself be surrounded by protection. Call upon me if you wish your nights to be safe from those energies that wish you harm.
Call upon me if you need to sleep in safety.
Call upon me if you wish your children to be safe during the day as well as the night.
Call upon me when you feel yourself in peril.
Call upon me when times are hard.
Call upon me when you need company, when you are lost and lonely.

I will be there when you call. For I can be everywhere in your world, whenever I'm needed. I am yours to call upon in times of need and comfort.

I am who I am.

Michael

***

December 1, 2014

Daily Message from the Angels and Ascended Masters

Amazing! You have spread across your world to find yourself, and yet you keep forgetting that you were never lost. We knew where you are non-stop. We are quite aware of where you've been, what you want out of life, and where you are heading. But you still go off on a tangent and say you are "looking for yourself".

Look in the mirror, child. Look in the mirror. Look at yourself deep in your eyes; see the depths of your very own soul. You are there. You aren't hidden; you aren't lost.

Let the Divine shower you with love, and you will realise you have found yourself in the same place you had left yourself. Right there in you, standing in front of that mirror.

Never say you are lost, for you will never be that. We watch over you.
Never say you are lonely, for we are always with you.
Never say you don't feel love, for we constantly shower you with it.
Never say you feel hate, for we won't allow it to consume you.
Never say you are ugly, for we find you beautiful and perfect, just the way you are.

And above all, never say you are useless, for we know of your little skills and talents, and we encourage you to use them. Darling ones, never give up. We won't let you fall.

I hear and see you all.

Hilarion

***

December 2, 2014

Daily Message from the Angels and Ascended Masters

The very stars in the sky and the earth you walk upon are all part of you. Cherish your world. It is you; the stars are you; the very plants are you. Even the humble sparrow is you.

Feel the life that lies within each living creature; they share the same life force as you. Feel the earth under your feet; its energies pulsate and travel within your body. That's because it is you.

So my darlings, why deny that you are above such magical and pure energies, and say you believe in science? Science is just words, but the Divine is life! You are life! You are all part of us, and we are part of you.

So much and so many, we love you.

Be well in life and be in peace with your own self.

Uriel

***

December 3, 2014

Daily Message from the Angels and Ascended Masters

Spiritual beings are more than just souls, more than just energies and more than just voices. We see them as receivers of knowledge, love and evolution.

Yes, you are more than just mediums and New Age people. You are the future of your world; see your world evolve around you and notice the differences you make. Every word and decision you make can make your world grow. Every thought makes things happen. They manifest. Choose wisely your thoughts and let them be thoughts of light. For in doing so, you make miracles happen.

Look in a mirror and see there's a miracle right there. You who have so much and yet are so unaware of how much you can do. That is what we are here to teach you about. The more you realise what wonders you can do, the more your world will rise in energies.

Open your minds and hearts; let us in them. Let us change the world together.

Thank you.

Uriel

***

December 4, 2014

Instead of a daily message, I was told to post this instead.

Whatever decision you have made in your life, it is yours to make, yours to keep, and yours alone. No one in your world has the right to unmake your decision. That is what free will is, and it was given to you to learn from. You alone can change your mind; no one else has that right. Be aware that this is one of your own personal powers.

You also have many other powers in your Divine will.

You have the power to love. This is an especially powerful ability, for it has no end, it has no beginning. In fact, it just is. When you love someone so much, you can move mountains, lift the heaviest weight, and in fact change the very world you are in with a thought. Love is what makes us all tick. It is what it is: the ultimate Divine power, and it was given to you and us.

Do what you want with it, for it is yours alone. Don't abuse it because it doesn't deserve that. Yet despite all its power, it is the gentlest power on your world. So why would you want to hurt it? For some petty power play? Some do, and in the end, karma pays them a visit. What you give out comes back to you threefold, including laughter, joy, peace, serenity, hope, and love.

That is what I need to talk about: the beautiful side of karma. And it is a beautiful side. For it is what karma was originally made for: to share the gifts you give to others, and to let others share their gifts with you. For in such ways of sharing and living, you are creating another aspect of love: harmony.

In harmony, you will create the future that you desire in your world: a world of peace, beauty, and tranquillity. All this is shared with the kingdom of nature. Sharing your world with the world of nature ensures that peace and harmony. It is your world too.

Are you not from the very depths of Nature herself? She is your ultimate mother, and Nature loves her children very much. Yes, Nature is harmony, peace, love, and joy.

The joy parts? Ah, yes, it is obvious, isn't it? Joy in the sight of a kitten finding its first steps. Joy in the sight of elephants bathing in a mud pool. Joy in seeing young birds learning to fly for the first time. Such is nature. Such is joy. And nature is joy, and very much so.

Such is the way of your world as it should be! No wars, no violence, no distrust or disruption. Those sorts of events are the tools of negative energies. They wish to control you, and so they create situations that demand you use negative energy to manipulate your environment.

The cure? Walk away from the situation. It's as simple as that! Walk away and leave it behind. It will only follow you if you allow it to do so, by carrying that negativity in your very being.

That is why I tell you to let it go and embrace the way of life as it should be: a life of light, peace, and love. That is all we want from you, for you will find happiness in such a life. Even if you don't think so, I assure you will. It is deep within you that such feelings will come.

Wash your hands and remove the stains of strife and pain. Wash your body and remove the marks of the struggles and torments in your life.

We all welcome you to your ultimate life of our light and love. All are waiting for you. You can come to this life any time, for no matter how much you delay it or are distracted, that door to peace is always open to you and will never close.

Come to us in love and be happy. Share the light, and we will look after you, healing you. Such is the light and the good side of karma as it should be, and it should rightfully be your destiny.

I am and always will so.

I AM!

When this presence arrived in my mind, I felt it had immense power. After I typed this out, I felt the presence leave my mind, and I ended up bawling my eyes out. Such emotions! Such power!

***

December 5, 2014

Daily Message from the Angels and Ascended Masters

Let a little laughter come into your life. If you feel down in the mouth and spirit, laugh at something silly. Once you start something as small as that initial chuckle, it pleases us. It means that you are starting to open. When the next sunny moment starts, you will laugh more. After all, once you start, the opportunities will keep coming. And then the climax of the whole situation? You will end up having a laugh over the whole thing.

Laughter is good for you; it is a form of exercise and heightens your vibrations, and we enjoy a good joke too. We will laugh with you. Laugh away your worries and let in the joy. Your outlook on your world will change for the better. And what better way than to laugh at life's jokes and silliness?

We all love you more when you laugh, anyway.

Haniel

***

December 6, 2014

Daily Message from the Angels and Ascended Masters

Beloved ones, why do you rush here and there with such impatience and anxiety? Why do you stress over such things that aren't worth your energy? Why start arguments over nothing? All of this isn't necessary but instead drains your light energy. This should not happen, but you let it. Not good at all.

Look at your problems with a neutral eye. Will you worrying about it create a solution? No? Then why worry? Instead, do some action on it and remove the problem. What sort of action is up to you? You can walk away from it, saying, "Why worry?" Or you can eliminate the problem by fixing it there and then. However you deal with it, stop worrying about the problem.

The only thing worrying got you was high blood pressure, low energies, stress and a headache. Are you arguing over nothing? If you feel someone is tormenting you into retaliation, walk away and calm down. You don't need this pressure in your life, and you will gain some consolation that this walking away annoys your antagonist more than your retaliation would. Don't stop and just keep walking away. Let karma deal with the irritations.

Are you rushing about? Why? Is the world going to end within the next two seconds? I don't think so. Take your time, enjoy the moment of mental solitude on your travels, and use it to contemplate on your dreams. Nothing is so urgent as to take your energies and lifestyle away from you. Nothing!

Even if you took your time, you'd get to your destination at the same time as if you had rushed it. What's the hurry?

I've had my say, and I shall let you think upon this.

With my love,

Jeremiel

***

December 7, 2014

Daily Message from the Angels and Ascended Masters

To those of you who don't realise what it is like within the light of the Divine, look within yourself and into the very core of your soul. There you will find the Divine light glowing within you bright and powerful. This is the real you. Feel the edges and then let that light race through you. Feel the exquisite power of such bounteous love and beauty. Such is the Divine light.

As you let it take over your inner self and surround you with its sweetness, you will then know what it is like. This is your own part of the Divine, and it is your connection to the Divine itself. For the Divine put part of its love within you.

When you let that inner light of yours infiltrate you to the DNA level, you are letting the Divine know you love it, and the Divine will return that love. Such inner light is part of the Divine's golden light.

Never think you are rejected by the Divine. You have never been rejected. The Divine is waiting for you to come to it.

Accept it, for it is beautiful, and so are you.

Be well.

Matriel

***

December 8, 2014

Daily Message from the Angels and Ascended Masters

Beautiful ones, be happy in your lot in life, for it is of your own choosing. Before your current incarnation, you chose the pattern of your life here. It is part of your lessons. If you are not happy in your current state, you can step away and move onto a new path. You have that choice.

No matter what you do in life, you should always know that we will support you in your choice. Do we have a choice in this ourselves? Yes. We chose to love you and will forever be with you. Don't ever forget that. We will be your strength, your love, your joy, and your hope.

You are our love, our hope, and our children. Isn't that good? Yes, it is. Remember that you are never alone, even in times of great peril. We will be with you.

Be well.

Jophiel

***

December 9, 2014

Daily Message from the Angels and Ascended Masters

As your world goes forward into a new future, it will take you with it, and you too are part of that new future. Prepare yourselves for an adventure that has never been seen by mankind. You will see the awakening of the sleepers within your populace. These sleepers are the peacemakers, the beacons of light, and the connectors of our children. You will know who they are when they show themselves.

They will bring themselves to your attention. Some of you can already see auras well; these sleepers will have an aura of the opal, and they shine in many colours.

These sleepers will bring you into a new age of light. This will be the new golden age, and it will last for millennia. They will bring you to the Divine light. The sleepers will soon arise. Prepare yourselves to head into a new era.

The Divine has spoken, and we all obey.

I await this event with much anticipation and love.

Ashtar

***

December 10, 2014

Daily Message from the Angels and Ascended Masters

Never forget where you come from. You come from the stars, you come from the breath of the Divine, and you come from the depths of the Divine's love. You are special beyond comprehension. To us, you are so perfect in our eyes, and you will forever be so. We love you without boundaries, and that too will forever be so.

Your soul and the angels are made from the same energies. The Divine made us all. We are one; we are kin. We are made with love, so never forget that. You are protected by us, as is fitting for us older spiritual kin. You are our younger siblings. You are perfect in our eyes, which I will repeat. Don't you dare forget it, for we will make sure you will be reminded repeatedly!

Never feel you are left out; never feel that you are forgotten. And never, ever feel unloved. You are loved for eternity.

Darling ones, we will welcome you with love and open arms when your time has come, giving love and joy in one embrace. Be well and show us that you can feel our love. Speak to us! We don't mind idle chit-chat or debates. We will listen. We will even join in if we wish.

I love you all.

I am Hilarion, with Gabriel at my side.

***

December 11, 2014

Daily Message from the Angels and Ascended Masters

Haven't you all been told to let go of all that holds you back? Told to release what no longer serves you? Yes, you have. But remember there are some things you must never let go: a memory of joy and laughter, your perfect self, a favourite tune, your personality, your ideas, your curiosity, your self-love, your unselfishness, and finally your love for each other.

These are what you must never let go or ruin. They are beautiful, they bring you happiness, and they belong to you. These special things make you your own person, for they are unique and pleasant.

Leave behind the clutter but keep the sweetness with you.

Jehudiel

***

December 12, 2014

Daily Message from the Angels and Ascended Masters

Beloved ones, do not forget your true selves, the part of you that stands tall, proud, and strong in the light. That part of you that is deep within you: your soul! Your soul is your true self. No matter what incarnation you go through, it remains constant and ever learning. This is you!

Your physical bodies are only temporary housing, but your immortal soul resides in each one of them. So do not fear death, for it is just a shedding of the physical form into your true light self. Your mind, consciousness, and personality are still there in your soul.

You see, you never will die. You will never become extinct while the light shines through you and on you. For after all, aren't you made of light too? Just like us!

So be proud and happy. You are of the Light, and that will give you immortality of a kind you never imagined.

Be well, dear ones, be well.

Michael

***

December 13, 2014

Daily Message from the Angels and Ascended Masters

Let the dark ego slip back and be part of your past. Instead, let the soul come through. The soul is all-caring and loving. It shines like a beacon. It is selfless, joyful, and giving.

The dark ego is selfish, cruel, hurtful, and controlling. You don't need that, for your soul is the opposite; it is made from the Divine's will. And nothing negative can touch that. In letting your soul come through, you are letting the Divine into your life. You are letting in the light.

Now, isn't that a beautiful thing?

Gabriel

***

December 14, 2014

Daily Message from the Angels and Ascended Masters

To who you believe your beloved ones be, be noted that they too are individuals. They too have their choices and their thoughts, and no one can change these for them. This rule goes for you too, for you have your own choices and thoughts, and no one has the right to change yours.

Please respect each other's decisions. It is their choice and theirs alone. If they involve you, you can choose to join in or not. If they don't, then step back.

The only time you may stop a person's choice is when it involves harm to innocents. The innocents did not choose to become involved.

Please be respectful of others and of your own choices, for they are what makes your path and destiny in life. The smallest decision can change worlds. Respect yourselves and each other. Give love when it is needed and heal when it is required.

This is our choice too.

Be well, beloved ones. I hear you.

Amael

***

December 15, 2014

Daily Message from the Angels and Ascended Masters

Do you believe in yourself? if not, why? Are you not made of truth and love? Are you not part of the Divine will? You exist, and you are what you are: proof that yourself is part of what is meant to be.

The entire world was ready for you all when you were created. And your path in life has many branches. We can only lead you to the diverted paths, but it is up to you as to what path you take. Each choice will mean a new change in your life and future. But the result is the same: you learn your lesson. The lesson you are given from the moment you agreed to incarnate again.

Yes, earth is your classroom, there is plenty of play time, and it is all mixed up with lessons. If you find your lessons and playtime are the same, then you have learnt your lesson well and are ready to grow. Even the poorest person in your world has a bit of time to play, even if it is a quick joke or looking at a picture. It is all part of life and learning.

Who are your teachers? You are your own teachers and own pupils. We simply hand out the lessons to which you agreed.

Be well, dearest ones. We shall talk again.

Calliel

***

December 16, 2014

Daily Message from the Angels and Ascended Masters

Believe in what you feel to be right. Your instincts will never let you down. Trust in yourself. You are the only one whom you can trust in your immediate surroundings.

Never let anyone take away your power, for it is yours alone. The people who try to take it are weak themselves and lack the trust you have.

Be strong in times of adversity, for those are the times when you are being tested. If you stand up to the pressures and rise successfully, then you have passed. If you flounder and weaken, falling by the wayside and running away, you have lost.

Be strong and believe in your own strength. For it is your spirit that is being tested, and when you win one test, you will find a door will open for you. It is a door towards a new step in your life path.

This is your reward.

Such as it is, we do reward those who show such strength and fortitude in times of discord, for they are the ones who will lead the new souls to their next step in life: growth. This is the reason why they were tested in the first place. If you are strong, you will be the other's tower to lean on. You will lead these people to their next path. And in times of chaos, you will protect them.

This is the way it is meant to be. I see strong people who think they can do this fall to the side. They did not follow their instincts and went for their own selfish purpose.

I have seen people who thought themselves weak suddenly stand up and take charge, saving a child's life. These are the people who are the strongest, for they chose to save another ahead of their own.

I am pleased by this because this selfless purpose is what I am aiming for. I am pleased with many of you, especially the mothers and fathers who cherish their children to the point of selflessness—and who bring up their children in the same way. Such is life as it is meant to be.

I love you all, my children, even the weakest of you all. To them I say you have yet to learn of your own inner strength, so prepare to learn and grow.

To harm others in the name of pleasure is not a strength. It is a perversion of spirit. This is not what you are meant to be, but you have made yourself. Time to grow up, time to let go of such things. For such people, I will repeatedly send them back until they learn from their mistakes. And when they do, then they can go forward. Such is the lot of the very young souls. They can be hedonistic until they start to grow up.

I do appreciate you are all reading and listening to me. My words echo within your very souls; though you say you don't hear me, your souls do. They hear every single word I say and will direct you to the way of the right.

I shall let you reflect and learn my words, for that is what I want you to do.

Believe in yourself, and to yourself be true.

I AM!

***

December 18, 2014

Daily Message from the Angels and Ascended Masters

A bit of knowledge for you all. Just when you thought you could go no further in your growth towards enlightenment, think again. You will never stop learning; you will always continue to grow. You just don't see it happening.

Your path in life is to grow and learn. The more you learn, the more you rise. In time, at the time of transition from your physical form to the energy form that is your soul, you will start to learn new knowledge and thoughts. This is normal because there are some things that you just can't learn in your world but can learn in ours.

Such knowledge is empowering. It gives you that added strength to the spirit within, making you stronger and more confident.

When you have learned all you can in your world and can't learn anything more, that's when ascension happens. And there begins a new lot of lessons that can only be learned on the spirit plane.

So be it, for it is a long path and a very interesting one.

Be well, dear ones.

Gabriel

***

December 19, 2014

Daily Message from the Angels and Ascended Masters

Dear ones, do you remember your childhood memories of your Christmas celebration? Do you remember the simple joy of a little, unexpected gift or visits from friends and family? The laughter and joy? Yes, you do. So why did you stop that joy and laughter and instead become so serious?

You say it's because of the expense of paying for the latest gadget or gift for the family. Has Christmas become so commercialized now? Don't spend all your funds on material goods that will go out of fashion within a few weeks. A waste of your precious time, I say. Instead, go back to the simpler ways of your childhood. Show your inner child a way out and let it run loose.

Remember how a simple jigsaw used to keep you entertained for a long time? A book went a long way, and above all, you were filled with joy!

That is what we want you to do: bring back that joy. That child within you is calling for it and will even bring more to you. And above all, never forget that Christmas is also a time for unconditional love for your fellow man. It's a time of laughter, peace, harmony, and fellowship.

Let it remain that way, not as a time of materialism, stress, and politics.

Be well, my dear ones,

Matriel and Raphael

***

December 20, 2014

Daily Message from the Angels and Ascended Masters

Give others their due when they give you a gift that is not monetary but of love. Give them their due by returning with a similar gift that is not physical but emotional—a gift of gratitude and love.

It's the same with us. We give you our gifts of love, joy, and comfort. We don't expect anything back, but we do find it pleasant if we receive love and gratitude back. It tells us that we are doing the right thing by you.

We thank you for that acknowledgement of our gifts to you. And we acknowledge you to be our own living gift from the Divine. Are we not all gifts from the Divine to each other?

Then it is so, and so it is.

Muriel

***

December 21, 2014

Daily Message from the Angels and Ascended Masters

Let the words flow from your lips—the words of joy, happiness, love, and laughter. Let these words begin your day as you start your work and when you head home. Don't let these words change within you. Embed them into your very soul. Become those words, and let the words become you.

You will in turn benefit from this, in that you will quietly and steadily believe in these words to the very core of you. The words will define your future and change your past.

These are words that you all need to follow in order to come closer to us. There are angels of infinite number who watch your path and see the changes within you. They will make sure that these changes will benefit you. They will make sure that you will grow into our midst.

Let them work with you in that aspect. Invite the angels into your life and home. Call them your spiritual family, for they are closer to you than your physical family. After all, they have watched over you since the birth of your soul.

Let them bring you to us, for once you have reached that certain level where the words have totally taken over you, we will bless you with our words and welcome you to our presence with open arms.

It will be such a beautiful sight to behold. So be it.

Osiris

***

December 22, 2014

Daily Message from the Angels and Ascended Masters

There is a time for laughter, there is a time for memories, and there is a time for love. Did you know there is a time for you alone? A time that you can just relax and be yourself. A time to pamper and spoil yourself.

Yes, there is! You all deserve that time. Set a rule in your household that at a certain time, you want to be alone with yourself. Use this moment to refresh, look after yourself, and just relax. This is your private moment to chill out. The maximum time per day should be an hour. If you have small children, let your partner take over for that time. If you are on your own, a friend, a relative, or a nursery can give you that little breathing space.

I have noticed that there are some who never take that time due to no help from any direction. My comment is, Shame on those who do not help these lonely people. Yes, I say lonely. For they never have the time to get in touch with us, their truest friends in the universe. Someone should help these lonely ones so that they can become friends to you and friends to themselves.

This is the season of giving. Give these lonely ones the gift of one hour of "me" time, and you will find that you will develop a long and trustworthy friendship. The result is that these lonely ones will no longer be lonely because they have now a friend: you.

Give them the gift of one hour, the gift of you!

I finish my words to you all and let you reflect.

Be well, dear ones.

Metatron

***

December 23, 2014

Daily Message from the Angels and Ascended Masters

As you go deeper into your meditations, open yourself up to us. Let us into your hearts and let us surround you with our love. Let this love draw into you, right to your very core. Relax and let our love surround you and merge with you at your atomic level.

As you do this, you feel changes within you. The changes feel warm, soft, gentle, and so pure. The changes are irreversible because they are part of the light.

Our love can change worlds and can change yours.

Let us love you with all our being. Feel our love envelope you, become part of you. And you become part of it.

Let the meditation continue while surrounded by this feeling inside and out of you. Soak in it. We love you unconditionally, and we want you to feel it. Our father loves you all. Be part of that too.

Forget the hurts and pains others have given you. That's in the past now. Our love is all now and the future.

When the time for your meditation is over, you will feel such peace and a sensation of completeness. We have cleansed you.

Be with our love.

Michael

***

December 24, 2014

Daily Message from the Angels and Ascended Masters

Are you ready?

Are you ready for the most wonderful thing in your entire planet? If not, you'd better get ready soon. Things are starting to happen. People are changing, worlds are changing, and your society is changing too. This change is called the shift, and your entire planet is heading into it. Some people don't understand and therefore create wars and disruption to control their world.

Too late! It's going to happen no matter how much you fight against it. There are many who will come through and become greater in their gifts. These are the ones who are ready and accepting of the change.

Those who reject this change are going to find themselves stuck in a world that they don't understand, and so they will find themselves left behind.

But it is nothing to worry about. Those who are left behind will eventually pass on and reincarnate. They will then find themselves back in this new world and will be very accepting of it. They will, in fact, love it.

No one is left behind permanently. As the world changes, so do you. Those who are fighting against it will change.

Stop fighting it; stop rejecting the change. You are in it, and it will happen. Accept it and enjoy the change.

You won't be disappointed, I assure you. And you will never be alone.

Be well.

Hilarion

***

December 25, 2014

Daily Message from the Angels and Ascended Masters

Now is the time for your celebration. You have food, drink, and gifts. You have family around you and are joining in with the festivities. But have any of you thought about those who have none of these? There are quite a few out there in your world.

Give those people a gift for this celebration. If it is a homeless person, let it be a gift of a blanket, clothing, a meal, or even a hot coffee. A little bit helps.

These people have no one left in the world to visit or rely on. They are truly alone. They have our company, but only a very few see or hear us. They have their minds on surviving.

Never forget those who are less fortunate than you. Give them a bit of your time; even if it is just for fifteen minutes, it is still something.

Be well, dear ones. Be well and pray to the Divine for love and peace. The Divine hears and sees all.

Emmanuel

***

December 26, 2014

Daily Message from the Angels and Ascended Masters

Just when you think it could get no worse and you are having dark thoughts. stop right there! You have hit rock bottom, and things can only go in one direction now: up!

Call upon us when you hit those bad moments. We will be around you faster than thought. We will send you our love. Reach out to us, and we will take your hand.

You are never alone and never will be. We will keep on telling you this until you finally accept it and believe it. And even then, we will keep telling you. You have our love for you, and that is never-ending. It is with love that we will help you, and it is with love that we will never leave you behind.

Accept that and believe it.

Do not ever despair when one door slams in your face. It simply means that the door is not a path you are meant to take. It is not part of your life lesson.

Accept that and believe it.

Be well, dear ones.

Emmanuel

***

December 27, 2014

Daily Message from the Angels and Ascended Masters

When will you all realise that you are all part of a much bigger picture in your world? Not everything revolves around you individually, as a single person has only himself or herself to rely on and therefore is a weaker force. Still strong, but not as much.

But all of you working together as one are extremely strong. You are all meant to be one, together in body and mind. You are meant to be that collective.

We too have that collective. Each single angel is strong as it is, but when we join in our collective, we are the force of the Divine's will. We are the stronger because we are the Divine's will. It was the Divine's will that made you and us. Together we are all stronger.

The single individual is not weak; it simply hasn't reached its full potential. The single angel is not weak; it is simply not at its full potential.

That is the collective.

I abide by what is meant to be. Join as one and be as one. One body, one mind, one soul. So be it.

Zadkiel

***

December 28, 2014

Daily Message from the Angels and Ascended Masters

Mighty is the pen, for it can write out the words of the soul and the heart. It can send these words out for all to hear. A pen can sing, do poetry, and express love. A sword can do none of these. It can only harm others.

Take heed of the lesson of the pen. Speak your words with love, music, and softness. Words can cure, heal, and bring together those who have parted in bad circumstances. Prepare to apologise for wrongs you did to others. Also, be prepared to forgive those who have wronged you.

Words are healing, and the intent can heal. Be careful what you say, for ego can take over, making the words cruel and hurtful. Leave behind that painful part of you. Ego likes to control you and use you. You are not meant to let it do that. Let your heart instead take over and heal rifts with your words.

Speak them now.

Words of regret? Change them to words of apology.

Words of hate? Change them into words of love.

So many changes in your life can happen when you do that, and all of these changes make you miraculous. For the changes are of the light.

Speak with loving thoughts and leave behind the bad thoughts. Let it happen, and you will never regret it.

Uriel

***

December 29, 2014

Daily Message from the Angels and Ascended Masters

Well, it is nearing the end of your current year. It has been an eventful one full of surprises—some good, some not so good. Such is the way of life.

There are good parts, and there are bad parts. Learn from the bad parts and use this new knowledge to help you reach the good parts more often. We only repeat a lesson if the student appears to be not learning it.

Soon it will be the start of a new year of lessons, adventures, and new knowledge. Learn from those too. For such is the way of life for you all. You must learn and then move on.

The new year will bring you many trials and many joyous moments. That is the way it is meant to be.

Be prepared for situations that appear to be out of your control, because those who have claimed to be leaders show that they are not.

It is time for you all to prepare for the changes that are coming. They are nearer than you think. New discoveries in the spiritual realm will come to those ready to learn from our side. There are new promises to be made.

As the time of the golden cat comes forward, so do the ones with the stars in on their foreheads come. They are the ones who will promise the world, but they are in fact bringers of the dreamers. The world is for them, and they will share it with all, for their way is the way of enlightenment.

Let it be so.

Matriel

***

December 30, 2014

Daily Message from the Angels and Ascended Masters

Do you believe in what is in front of you and can only be seen with your own eyes? Why do you limit yourself to such a viewpoint? Your universe has many wonders, and in its vastness, there are more things than you can ever imagine. There are things that your mind, at its current level of evolution, cannot understand.

When you restrict your own imagination to material thoughts, you are running away from the vast, amazing beauty that is beyond your world. You are hiding, closing yourself off from others and yourself. That is not good, for you are all made to seek out the wonders of the universe. You are made to learn and grow within its many wonders.

Did you know that you are one of its many wonders? Well, you do now. Be happy with that knowledge. You were all born to seek out the truth and the light. Seek it out, learn it, admire it, and live it.

So why hide? It's too beautiful to turn away from, so go and seek it.

Let it be so.

Emmanuel

***

December 31, 2014

Daily Message from the Angels and Ascended Masters

Now, remember what may come to you will be either a gift from us or a lesson to be learned. A lesson is always found in every situation that is around you. See what happens! What can you do? What can you say? What can it teach you? These are the lessons. When you have learnt the lesson that is given and find you have come to a solution that is beneficial to you, that is when you get your gift.

Your gifts and lessons come in many shapes and sizes. Some can even be the same. Nothing is cut and dried, as you say.

Be patient and study the situation before you join in it. That way you will find the solution easier to work with.

Gifts? Lessons? We have them all. Our love is our gift to you. Your gift to us is you.

Be well, dearest ones, be well.

Let no harm come to you or your family.

Chamuel

The End

www.ingramcontent.com/pod-product-compliance
Lightning Source LLC
Chambersburg PA
CBHW030258080526
44584CB00012B/357